"Keep your highlighter handy! This book is brilliant—rich in wisdom, inviting in style and logical in structure. It is immensely, practically and immediately helpful. I'll admit my biases: great admiration for Gayle Beebe, huge respect for Peter Drucker and a warm friendship with the publisher, Inter-Varsity Press. Of any recent book on leadership, and there are many, I want this one close at hand."

JOHN D. BECKETT, chairman, The Beckett Companies, author of *Loving Monday* and *Mastering Monday*

"I am so thankful for Gayle Beebe. I am confident that you will share my gratitude for him when you have completed reading *The Shaping of an Effective Leader.* In this wise, practical and insightful book, Beebe serves as a trustworthy guide for helping us understand the meaning and expectations of leadership. Readers will gain a greater appreciation for the work of leaders and leadership teams, as well as the key aspects of effective organizations. I learned much from this book and heartily commend it to others."

DAVID S. DOCKERY, president, Union University

"This marvelous book on leadership is a product of Dr. Beebe's creative thinking and research, as well as his effective use of leadership concepts from other professional thinkers. The bottom line is this book is filled with challenging new ideas presented with great clarity. Whether you are just beginning your career, are a professional coaching top executives or have already achieved a significant leadership position, you will benefit from reading this insightful book. There is much for all of us to learn about leadership. Those willing to look critically into the mirror of this book will unquestionably become more effective leaders."

WILLIAM T. ESREY, retired chair and CEO, Sprint

"This is not just another book on leadership. It is written by an effective leader who has achieved meaningful results in the organizations he has led. He shares with us lessons and principles he has learned from the mentoring relationships he had with Peter Drucker and other important thought leaders. It was Drucker who reminded us that a leader has only one choice to make—to lead or mislead. Gayle Beebe has chosen to lead. Read and learn from his wisdom and experience."

C. WILLIAM POLLARD, chairman emeritus, ServiceMaster

"This book is for all individuals, organizations, schools and businesses, profit and nonprofit. During this time when leadership in political and industrial arenas has deteriorated, Beebe's book shows and develops the importance of maintaining clear convictions as we lead. The 'pyramid' of conditions for developing strong leadership makes it easy to discern where and how one is starting and where one is going. Complex ideas are put in understandable terms: 'Decisions are choices between alternate courses of action.'"

LESLIE RIDLEY-TREE, president and CEO, Pacific Air Industries

Every person who serves in leadership or aspires to needs to read this book. . . . This book instructs without being pedantic, inspires without being clichéd and challenges without being arrogant. It reminds us that leadership is not only an art; it is a practice to be nurtured, cultivated and honed over a lifetime. Because the book frames the leadership experience in such helpful and formative ways, someone aspiring for insight born of experience and rigorous thinking will find a reservoir of valuable wisdom."

DR. STEVE MOORE, executive director and CEO, The M. J. Murdock Trust

THE
SHAPING OF
AN EFFECTIVE
LEADER

Eight Formative Principles
of Leadership

Gayle D. Beebe

Foreword by Steve Forbes

IVP Books

An imprint of InterVarsity Press
Downers Grove, Illinois

InterVarsity Press
P.O. Box 1400, Downers Grove, IL 60515-1426
World Wide Web: www.ivpress.com
E-mail: email@ivpress.com

InterVarsity Press® is the book-publishing division of InterVarsity Christian Fellowship/USA®, a
movement of students and faculty active on campus at hundreds of universities, colleges and schools
of nursing in the United States of America, and a member movement of the International Fellowship
of Evangelical Students. For information about local and regional activities, write Public Relations
Dept., InterVarsity Christian Fellowship/USA, 6400 Schroeder Rd., P.O. Box 7895, Madison, WI
53707-7895, or visit the IVCF website at <www.intervarsity.org>.

Red Poling's management philosophy, found on p. 87, is used by permission of Harold A. "Red" Poling.
All rights reserved.

Design: Cindy Kiple

ISBN 978-0-8308-3820-2

Printed in the United States of America ∞

Library of Congress Cataloging-in-Publication Data

Beebe, Gayle D.
   The shaping of an effective leader: eight formative principles of leadership / Gayle D. Beebe.
      p. cm.
   Includes bibliographical references and index.
   ISBN 978-0-8308-3820-2 (pbk.: alk. paper)
   1. Leadership. 2. Leadership—Moral and ethical aspects. 3.
Drucker, Peter F. (Peter Ferdinand), 1909-2005. I. Title.
   HD57.7.B433 2011
   658.4'092—dc23

2011032882

| P | 18 | 17 | 16 | 15 | 14 | 13 | 12 | 11 | 10 | 9 | 8 | 7 | 6 | 5 | 4 | 3 | 2 |
| Y | 25 | 24 | 23 | 22 | 21 | 20 | 19 | 18 | 17 | 16 | 15 | 14 | 13 | 12 | 11 | | |

This book is dedicated to my father,
Richard H. Beebe (1928-1989),
who is always present, though no longer here;
and to the members of the executive teams
with whom I have served:

Spring Arbor University
Betty Overton-Adkins
Matt Osborne
Doug Jones
Reed Sheard
Kim Hayworth
Jay Mansur
Tim Johnston
Brad Sydow
Damon Seacott

Westmont College
Rick Pointer
Chris Call
Doug Jones
Reed Sheard
Jane Higa
Cliff Lundberg
Bill Wright
Steve Baker
Warren Rogers
Nancy Town

CONTENTS

FOREWORD

We live in an era when, as never before, the true source of wealth and capital for an economy is not physical but metaphysical. The human mind's inventiveness and spirit of innovation enables us to move forward and achieve an ever higher standard of living. The so-called information age began with the microchip. In days of old, people thought wealth meant large tracts of land and massive armies. But what is a microchip? Silicon, which is sand. There is no shortage of sand in this world.

Look around the world and you quickly see that the economies that move ahead impressively don't do it by depending on natural resources. They do it by allowing individuals to develop their entrepreneurial instincts. There is no shortage in the world of people scrambling to get ahead. But the challenge is to create the institutions that foster a free market environment, which enables these energies to create countless new businesses that innovate and grow.

We must recognize there is a moral foundation to commerce: you succeed by meeting the needs and wants of other people. Even if you think you're in it for yourself, you don't succeed unless you meet the desires of your customers. If you're not willing to take risks, you're not going to get ahead. Misers—people who simply clutch what they have in a selfish way à la Ebenezer Scrooge—do not go out and found the Walmarts, the Microsofts and the Googles of the world. They simply live a narrow and constricted existence.

This leads to the importance of leadership and the moral foundations it must create. We think of economics as just about material things, but if we don't have a strong sense of what is right and wrong, commerce ultimately comes to a halt—at least, progress comes to a halt. We need an environment where people can take risks, which means the rule of law, where people have a sense of right and wrong. If they don't, the system doesn't work. It's based on trust.

We need a strong moral foundation as we reach out into the world. We've had periods of great spurts of globalization before, particularly from the end of the Napoleonic Wars to the First World War. But from that catastrophe and the subsequent Great Depression came the rise of totalitarian ideologies: Communism, Fascism and Nazism. We defeated Nazism and Fascism with the Second World War. We thought we finally defeated the last of these—Communism—with the end of the Cold War. But now we're facing another kind of fanaticism in the world. If you look at the ideologies of those extremists today, you find a lethal mix of Marxism, Nietzsche-like nihilism and Fascism. Without the kind of moral foundation and values that lie at the heart of great leadership, the world will ultimately destroy itself, and civilization will go into a new dark age.

Gayle Beebe's book is valuable precisely because it discusses how effective and moral leaders develop. Leaders in all spheres of society set the moral tone for their organizations. Thus the book begins by establishing the importance of a moral foundation for all of life—and especially for the leaders who influence our lives. Then, drawing upon one of civilization's truly great geniuses,

Gayle wonderfully applies the insights of Peter Drucker, his former professor and the father of modern management theories.

Drucker's genius arose from a combination of intense curiosity, moral principles and a keen perceptiveness of the perfections and imperfections of human nature. During his long and distinguished life, he never went stale intellectually, which is why business journalists, executives, entrepreneurs, leaders of nonprofit institutions, students and the occasional wise politician eagerly sought his thoughts right up to the time he died. Drucker possessed a profound understanding of economics. He was deeply influenced by a fellow Austrian, Joseph Schumpeter. Schumpeter coined the term "creative destruction," a trademark phrase that brought a wry smile to Drucker's face. It underscored the enduring importance of leaders acting like entrepreneurs in order to create new value for their companies. Drucker repeatedly emphasized the necessity of carving out time to think, determining not only what to do but also what to stop doing. Drucker urged leaders to stay focused on two or three of the most important things and delegate the rest to others. He was the first to recognize the emergence of workers whose most important asset is the knowledge they carry in their heads.

Drucker wrote thirty-nine books and published hundreds of articles and interviews. His work made a major impact on modern organizations throughout the second half of the twentieth century. This legacy will continue to influence every new generation of leaders, as it should. Gayle Beebe's effort to capture the essence of this impact is a wonderful contribution to the chorus of voices that recognize Drucker as the most formative and far-ranging thinker in the modern history of management. May this contribution endure, and may you enjoy the read.

Steve Forbes

PREFACE

"I Think He Said His Name Is Peter"

It was a little past eight on a Monday night. After enjoying a simple dinner with my wife, Pam, I had settled into the back bedroom of our modest apartment for a long night of homework. Now the phone was ringing. As Pam answered the call I could hear her struggling to understand the voice on the other end. *Another telemarketer*, I thought to myself. After a brief exchange on the phone, the door to our back bedroom swung open and, with a puzzled look on her face, Pam said, "There's someone on the phone for you; I think he said his name is Peter."

My mind began to race. *Could this be Dr. Drucker?* I wondered. Even though he had encouraged us to write him questions at the end of class, I didn't believe he would call me on the phone to follow up. As I picked up the receiver and offered a simple greeting, I heard a familiar voice with a thick Viennese accent reply, "Good evening, this is Peter Drucker." Peter—he always insisted we call him Peter—had called in response to my question and was now inviting me to join him for lunch to discuss it further. The following Friday we met at Griswald's Restaurant in Claremont, California, and began a series of encounters that would become the most formative influence on my philosophy of leadership.

That first encounter at Griswald's remains so memorable because it reflected Drucker's keen interest in his students. We talked about his friendship with "Dick" (H. Richard) Niebuhr, his translation of Kierkegaard and his love of St. Bonaventure. When I shared with him what I was reading in my Ph.D. program, he teased me about studying the "modern heretics." Ultimately, he talked to me about giving back, about the responsibility we all carry to make a contribution. I am forever grateful.

As a result, this book is both a tribute to Peter Drucker and an opportunity to consider together why leaders matter and how each of us can develop a level of effectiveness that ensures our success. For most of us, our early forays into leadership responsibilities happen without a lot of forethought. In my case, prior to studying with Drucker, I had no real sense of how to understand and execute my own responsibilities as a leader.

In 1985, when I accepted my first major leadership position, I struggled to understand my work. There were few defined expectations. Nobody told me how to approach my job or how to manage myself in fulfilling these responsibilities. There were no instructions on when to go to bed, how to manage my time or whom I should hire. Despite attending one of the finest graduate schools in the entire country, I had not taken a single class in how to run an organization, build a budget or develop a strategic plan. Yet, as I did my work, these were the very skills that were expected of me. It was then that I began to read and study the principles of leadership.

During these early years I was given a copy of *The Effective Executive*, Drucker's timeless classic on the nature of leadership.[1] I was mesmerized by the way Drucker provided a comprehensive view of the work of an executive. My experience with this book triggered an interest in studying with him, and over time I realized why he earned the title "the father of modern management."

In 1990, Pam and I moved from a bedroom community of Portland, Oregon, to Southern California so that I could pursue a dual degree (a Ph.D. in the philosophy of religion and an MBA in strategic management) at Claremont Graduate University (CGU), the graduate school of the five Claremont colleges (Pomona, Claremont McKenna, Harvey Mudd, Scripps and Pitzer). Offering the only program of its type in the country, CGU allows a motivated student to pursue a Ph.D. by day and an MBA by night.[2] As a result, I often found myself studying Hegel, Husserl or Aquinas in the morning and analyzing spreadsheets, discussing case studies or considering economic policies by night. Four of my classes were with Drucker, always during the same three-hour block on Mondays, always without breaks.[3]

To encounter Peter Drucker through a class, a conversation or a book was to be drawn into the great questions every leader must answer. Drucker rarely provided rote answers to a particular situation.[4] His great contribution was teaching his students and associates how to think by asking them timeless questions to guide their understanding.

As a result, Drucker's questions dominate my mind every time I make a decision. What is the role of politics in building an executive team? How can I structure my time into "blocks" so as to consolidate my concentration and be more effective? Why do the people I hire immediately share my philosophy of leadership and vision for the organization while the executives I inherit always take more time? Although as a leader I need to spend most of my time at the strategic level, when should I reach down into the operational level, thus honing my awareness of how the priorities of the organization are being carried out? Ultimately, what makes for an effective executive?

Another great lesson I learned from Drucker was the difference between activity and results. He had an uncanny ability to point out how frequently we mistake activity for results, never stopping to ask if the activities we are pursuing are going to generate the results we desire. As a result, he remains one of the most insightful and provocative writers on leadership precisely because he questions a leader's natural biases, thereby keeping the focus on the right challenges in order to achieve the right results.

By the time I finished studying at Claremont, my career in higher education was well underway and my general framework for thinking through leadership was taking shape. To my great joy, I have loved every minute of it. What the dual degree, and especially the MBA, did for me is immeasurable. It accelerated my opportunities in a field that traditionally has been skeptical of business practices but that recently has come to recognize and rely on them. Part of what I enjoy in Drucker's philosophy of leadership is that his approach honors the individual leader while insisting that the ultimate measurement of a leader's success is the contribution he or she makes to the broader purposes of an organization.

Beyond all the lectures, case studies and conversations, one dominant memory rises: watching one of the greatest business minds of all time rove across vast arrays of human knowledge, gleaning insights, providing explanations and producing a synthesis that was always ahead of its time. Seeing Drucker's mind work remains one of the most enjoyable and enriching experiences of my entire life. And in seeing his mind work, I learned the unique work of leadership as well.

In addition to learning how to lead, I was touched by his life. I noticed his respectful treatment of the support staff—of Elizabeth, the faculty secretary whom he treated graciously, and of Jose, the janitor who cleaned Albrecht Auditorium, whom he always greeted by name. Of all the prominent people I have known, Drucker always seemed to have time for the common person. He talked a great deal about treating everyone with integrity, care and respect; seeing such treatment modeled deepened the impact of his words.

On November 11, 2005, I was walking down Seventh Avenue in midtown Manhattan when I learned of his death. As I neared the ESPN Zone, its giant neon sign announced, "Peter Drucker, the father of modern management, is dead at the age of 95." He was just a week shy of his ninety-sixth birthday. We knew he was beginning to fail physically, but his intellectual capacity had seemed undimmed. Just as his life had begun at the start of the twentieth century, it ended as we were entering an era he had anticipated and in many respects helped to define. During the twentieth century he gave the world a new understanding of the work of leadership and the essential role it must play in managing the complexity of organizations that define the twenty-first century. He also gave us the gift of his life. What a century; what a life!

INTRODUCTION

Eight Principles of Effective Leadership

Leaders matter. The fortunes of every organization, whether great or small, rise and fall based on the effectiveness of its leadership. Whether you are the head of a large company, or a mid-level manager responsible for a single division, or even a single employee in a start-up company, what you do as a leader fundamentally shapes the destiny of your organization. How then do we become effective leaders?

My philosophy of effective leadership developed over time. It began as I accepted early opportunities to hold different leadership positions. It expanded when I went to study with Peter Drucker. As I progressed in my work and was offered increasing levels of responsibility, I reached out to key mentors who provided guidance and support. Eventually, I recognized the contribution high-quality academic programs could play in my own development. Ultimately, this constellation of great academics, key mentors and multiple leadership experiences refined my sense of what made a difference and what didn't matter at all. This transformed my understanding.

I am now in my twelfth year as a college president. My first seven years as a president were spent at Spring Arbor University in Michigan. During that time, we nearly doubled the enrollment (2,400 to over 4,000 students), added fifteen new academic programs and built eleven new buildings while renovating fifteen others. For the past five years I have been president of Westmont College in Santa Barbara, California, a nationally ranked liberal arts college with a specific focus on high-quality undergraduate education. Prior to becoming a president, I held various mid-level leadership positions in other nonprofits as well as being a dean, director and department chair at a large university for eight years. Today, as president of Westmont College, my primary responsibility is to lead and manage an organization that employs a vast array of highly talented people, while serving the educational needs of our students. How then can I lead effectively and achieve desirable results?

The goal of this book is to identify and articulate the eight principles of effective leadership. In many respects Drucker's life and work exemplified these principles, and my goal is to demonstrate how their successful development and implementation can make such an important difference in leadership. The eight principles of effective leadership are illustrated in figure 0.1.

This diagram is both descriptive and prescriptive. It identifies the way leadership develops and prescribes the way each of us can make a difference through our leadership.

As we progress in our development, each rank of the pyramid is built on what went before. In other words, *character* is the foundation of all leadership responsibilities for all our life.

Then, *threshold competencies*, built on our character, determine enduring effectiveness. I place threshold competencies second because a moral leader can only be effective if he or she has the competency to manage all the other levels of the organization.

Next, *team chemistry* is absolutely essential. The capacity of any management team and its ability to function effectively will be

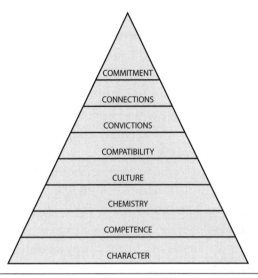

Figure 0.1. The eight principles of effective leadership

built on the character of each individual and the range of skills and abilities he or she brings to each task.

Likewise, the *organizational culture* of the company is built on the relationships and priorities that are established with all members of the organization. Those who produce the organizational culture are also responsible for interfacing with the broader environmental context.

As the culture develops, moreover, each individual must determine the level of *compatibility* between his or her personal goals and values, and the goals and values of the organization.

Likewise, the *convictions* we develop about what should be done and how it should be accomplished are built on the five previous levels of development.

Then, remaining *connected* to our work associates even when we make hard decisions is only possible if we maintain personal integrity, display competence, create team chemistry, develop a great culture, retain a level of compatibility that motivates, and display a level of conviction and commitment that create both a dependability and predictability that people trust.

Finally, making an *ultimate contribution* that will outlive us is only possible when these seven previous stages are successfully fulfilled. If any one of these stages collapses, the effectiveness of our leadership will retreat to this level, and we will need to start all over again. In the case of a moral failing, it is virtually impossible to ever recover completely.

My understanding of how effective leaders develop and why they matter began initially when I was attending a workshop being led by a man who had ruined one organization and was in the process of ruining another. He was extolling the singular importance of character when I realized that without threshold competencies even the most well meaning individual can do real harm. As I was listening, I began to outline the progressive principles of leadership development and began to realize how effective leaders develop and make an important difference through their work.

During this time I also realized that our understanding of leadership does not come to us all at once. It takes time. In our instant-oriented culture we often want to short-circuit the thinking, reflecting and acting that mark our progressive development as leaders. Understanding how leaders develop and why they matter requires discernment, wisdom and insight.

Because effective leadership is both an art and a science, there is more than one right way to lead. The way we understand and apply these principles will be based on our own gifts, abilities and judgment. Still, it is incumbent that we learn how to combine an understanding and development of these eight principles with their application in the specific contexts we face.

In order to understand how each principle develops, I begin every chapter with a story illustrating how the specific principle came to light in the midst of leadership. Then, I consider Drucker's extensive treatment of this principle and demonstrate its importance with specific examples from real life. After considering Drucker's teaching, I amplify each principle by considering the way I learned it, including the ongoing influence of one or two key mentors on my own life and leadership. An added element is the identification and application of the eight deadly vices and the eight life-giving virtues to each level of the pyramid in order to illustrate how our character is tested and developed as we assume new and higher levels of responsibility over time. Finally, each chapter concludes with a consideration of how the particular principle needs to be developed further in our current leadership responsibilities in order to accomplish effectiveness and ensure success.

Ultimately, it is my hope that this book will help you understand how leaders develop and why their ongoing development is so important. Above all, this work is both an invitation to understand and develop as a leader and an encouragement to engage in the rich and noble privilege of providing leadership for an organization at whatever level you may serve.

Principle 1

THE NECESSITY
OF CHARACTER

The Foundation of Effective Leadership

The final proof of the sincerity and seriousness of management is
uncompromising emphasis on integrity of character. For it is
character through which leadership is exercised;
*it is character that sets the example **and is imitated**. Character is not some-*
thing one can fool people about.

Peter Drucker

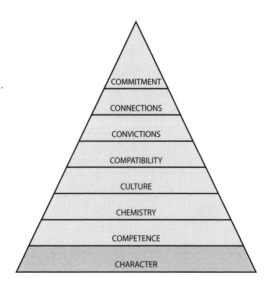

"It all comes down to ethics," replied the former CEO of a multi-billion dollar investment company. We were golfing at The Quarry in La Quinta, California, and I had just asked him what he thought was the secret of success in life and business. Our minds had drifted to the case of Bernie Ebbers at WorldCom, then to Ken Lay at Enron and finally to Bernie Madoff and others. The list seemed endless as we considered one unethical leader after another whose corrupt practices had led their companies into bankruptcy. As we neared the end of our round, he turned and asked, "What are you doing to teach ethics to the next generation of students?"

Twenty-five hundred years ago, Plato (427-347 B.C.) pondered the same question. "Can you tell me, Socrates, is virtue something that can be taught? Or does it come by practice? Or is it neither teaching nor practice that gives it to a man but natural aptitude or something else?"[1] Throughout this long and provocative dialogue, Plato eventually concludes that virtue is only developed in people who commit their entire lives to realizing it.

As Plato notes, through education, discipline, natural aptitude and hard work we discover the benefits of the virtuous life and of committing our lives to a wisdom tradition that can guide us. We also realize that the purposes behind every effort at education must include moral purposes. In discovering these moral purposes we realize that every generation must receive guidance if its members are to discover the ultimate destiny of their lives and the ultimate contributions they can make as leaders.

I have seen so many great leaders ruin an opportunity because of a moral failing. Sometimes it has been the ruinous vices of committing moral indiscretions, embezzling money or practicing corrupt politics. More often than not, however, it has been the lesser evils that simply undermine people's confidence in these leaders' work.

Years ago when I was a dean, I was working with a man who had an inability to control his temper. He would get angry with himself and his circumstances, and in the midst of his anger lash out at those around him. In one telling scene he completely destroyed his opportunity when he blew up at his board of directors and said derogatory and destructive things about them that forever undermined their ability to trust him. Shortly thereafter, he was fired from his position and never worked again in this line of work. It wasn't a deadly vice that did him in, but the inability to exercise emotional intelligence.

During this episode, I couldn't help but think about how each of us has an area of vulnerability that often prevents us from realizing our full potential. Many of us struggle in specific areas that keep us from being all that we could be. Learning how to identify and overcome our most self-destructive tendencies plays an indispensable role in our enduring success.

On Character

Character is built on our understanding of ethics. In Western society there are at least seven major streams of ethical theory that still inform us: virtue ethics, deontological ethics, utilitarian ethics, contractual ethics, communitarian ethics, feminist ethics and postmodern ethics. Ethical theories encompass and express wisdom traditions. Wisdom traditions, in turn, often evoke longings and guiding principles that tie our individual lives into purposes greater than ourselves. Our capacity to build a foundation based on character will determine the extent to which we can achieve long-term, sustainable success.

Although these seven dominant streams still inform us, more recent attention has shifted to developmental psychology and especially the stages of moral development. A guiding resource in this development is Lawrence Kohlberg's landmark study *Theories of Moral Reasoning*.[2] Identifying and outlining the six primary stages of moral development, Kohlberg made the astonishing claim that 80 percent of all Americans live at either a stage three level (acquiescence to cultural norms) or a stage four level (obedience to law and order) of moral reasoning, depending on their vision of the moral life.

Peter Drucker, too, worked from a moral vision, using what he calls the "mirror test." This test asks a quite basic question: Whom do you want to see in the mirror when you wake up in the morning—a morally upright and respected person or an individual devoid of a soul?

Throughout his long and distinguished career, Drucker both articulated and assumed the necessity of character formation. He often emphasized that there is no such thing as "business ethics"— a person is either ethical or unethical, regardless of the situation. He insisted, moreover, that bedrock integrity was absolutely necessary for effective leadership.

I continue to be struck by this emphasis. Throughout my leadership I have often seen young, promising executives derailed by the most pernicious character flaws. These events have had little to do with these executives' competence and everything to do with their lack of character.

Drucker amplifies the importance of integrity by noting that the greatest test of our integrity and character is the way we treat other people. In *Management*, Drucker writes, "They may forgive a man a great deal: incompetence, ignorance, insecurity, or bad manners. But they will not forgive his lack of integrity."[3] He goes on to emphasize that a person's lack of integrity is so serious that if it is discovered, it should immediately disqualify him or her from any position of leadership.[4]

Drucker also expresses concern that a manager's attention needs to be focused on the strengths, not the weaknesses, of those he or she is responsible for. He repeatedly emphasizes the importance of making our strengths dominant and our weaknesses irrelevant. He believed this was the unique responsibility of the leader and reflected the nature of the leader's character. He believed great leaders understood their people, but this understanding was not so that they could eliminate everyone who didn't measure up. This understanding helped a leader focus on an individual's strengths, not their weaknesses, and led to Drucker's participation and interest in the StrengthsFinder movement.[5]

Drucker's primary focus included the responsibility of developing those people under a leader's care. Noting that every one of us comes to a position of leadership with gifts and limitations, Drucker emphasized that our basic integrity and character are displayed in our willingness to develop other people. In his own fitting way Drucker summed up the importance of integrity and character by noting, "The manager who lacks character—no matter how likeable, helpful, or amiable, no matter how competent or brilliant—is a menace and should be judged unfit to be a manager and a gentleman."[6]

Though it may sound extreme, Drucker's point is this: why put up with jerks? Life is too short and our work too hard to endure people who are merely out to ruin us.

Ultimately, Drucker believed the moral tone for the entire organization starts at the top. He believed, and I think he is right, that the behavior of senior executives fundamentally sets the tone for an organization.[7] He amplifies this by noting that our people decisions must demonstrate that we will be unwavering in insisting that leaders at all levels of the organization must have basic integrity that can be trusted. It is simply too crucial and cannot be acquired later. This is also why moral failings are so catastrophic: they undermine the very trust that is at the heart of leadership.[8]

Drucker's point is that organizations rely on the character of the people who run them. Our strategy decisions, our people decisions and even our resource decisions have to be made by people who are honest and operate with integrity. Otherwise, the consequences are disastrous. They aren't always immediate, but eventually, over time, organizations that lack integrity fall apart. The implosions of WorldCom, Enron and Madoff Investment Securities did not happen immediately. Their deceitful strategies worked for a long time, but inevitably, when the economy imploded, the men behind them were exposed for their fraud.

Why Character Counts and How Character Develops

But why worry about our character? The formation of our character creates predictability to our leadership. Predictability, dependability and consistency: these three qualities ensure that our leadership is reliable and motivates people to place their confidence in us. Our effectiveness as leaders is built on trust. Though more than 75 percent of Americans surveyed by the Gallup Poll admitted they would lie, cheat or steal if they thought they could get away with it, the leader is on constant display and cannot escape the spotlight of public scrutiny.

Our goal for the first principle of effective leadership is to identify and illustrate the natural and deliberate processes of character formation. Character formation establishes the foundation for great leadership success. When absent, it charts the path for colossal leadership failure. Because our character is formed by our beliefs, actions, self-reflection on our actions and corrective behaviors as a result of this self-reflection, we must recognize the way these beliefs, actions and reflections both shape and reflect our character.

One of the great challenges facing a new leader is developing the capacity for moral self-reflection. So often what distinguishes great leaders from also-rans is whether or not we can develop a capacity to self-correct. Leaders get off track. We overreact. We walk into situations and do not respond as we should. This in and of itself is usually not a problem. It becomes a problem when we cannot recover from our mistakes. The first step to recovering from our mistakes is to recognize we made them.

One of the great examples of how to develop the capacity for self-reflection and self-correction is taken from the famous scene in Shakespeare's *Hamlet* where Hamlet reenacts the murder of his father in order to "catch the conscience of the King." What this passage so poignantly demonstrates is that the capacity for self-reflection and self-correction can keep us from the path of self-destruction. Otherwise, left to our own devices, we will fall into patterns governed by self-interest that come to rule us.

Often, our own moral awakening results from our confrontation with the fact that we are completely out of sync with our deeply held convictions. When we recognize this, the next step is to realize how to get back on course: by elevating our deepest convictions and pursuing our principles from a new perspective. So often leaders have to go through a moral reorientation in which they come to see their present reality in a completely new light. Parables, or stories meant to teach a moral lesson, prompt us to reflect on our life by seeing our life in motion. Through encountering a very basic, common reality they invite us to take an entirely new look at life.

Once we recognize that we are out of sync and need to improve our performance, we can engage in the sort of development that inspires people to follow us. Individuals want to know that they can rely on us. If they trust the way we lead, and it is successful, then they will also be interested in the way we recover from mistakes. Together, our strategies for success and our recovery from failures will give people the confidence to trust us, and subsequently we will have the moral authority to lead well.

Realistically, however, it is very difficult if not impossible to lead well and recover nobly without the help of others. The input of older, wiser individuals who can guide our development is often needed. Two individuals who have played a key role in my own character formation are Richard Foster and Diogenes Allen. I first met Foster in 1977 when he was teaching at the university I attended and was in the midst of writing *Celebration of Discipline.*

About once a month he would distribute chapters to several students, asking us to read and respond to his work. This early introduction to his writing electrified me. It created a deep desire to devote my life to this inner dimension where our character develops and our motives for acting are formed. In addition, Foster was willing to meet with us one-on-one and ask us questions about our own development that nobody else was willing to ask. To this day, I still enjoy the opportunity to be with him as he conducts a Socratic inventory of my inner self.

Five years later I enrolled at Princeton Theological Seminary, where I pursued a master's of divinity degree (1982-1985). Shortly after arriving, one of my favorite mentors died, and I was at a loss to understand the nature of life, especially the challenge of evil and suffering in our world. In the midst of this tragedy, I met Diogenes Allen, Stuart Professor of Philosophy and a former Rhodes Scholar, who had just published a book on suffering.

Our initial meeting revealed his remarkable gifts, abilities and sensitivities. Allen took my concerns seriously. He directed me to key texts that influenced my understanding of the problem of evil and suffering. He invited me to take part in his philosophy class the following spring, when he planned to discuss these topics further. Most importantly, he spent time with me, helping me understand the nature of evil and suffering, and the importance of redeeming our suffering so as not to become embittered.

During my final year at Princeton I wrote my master's thesis with Allen. The topic was moral philosophy and, specifically, the work of Iris Murdoch. A key piece of Ms. Murdoch's philosophy is "visionary ethics," the belief that people behave according to the vision of life they are pursuing. As helpful as following rules and commands may have been in the past, Murdoch's emphasis on a vision of life and the way this can move us from an egocentric outlook to a reality-centered outlook has forever shaped me.

By investing substantial time in me, Foster and Allen played an indispensable role in my intellectual and moral development. In particular, they helped me recognize the role that our thoughts, habits and dispositions play in shaping our character. They also introduced me to key thinkers who deepened my understanding. Two, in particular, are especially important: Erik Erikson and Evagrius of Pontus.

Erik Erikson, Evagrius and Our Development as Leaders

I like to know the "why" of something before I'm willing to do the "how." In other words, I want to know why character formation is important before I am interested in how it happens. When I arrived at Princeton in 1982, I had become convinced that integrity is the foundation of life; I believed that choosing to be ethical and true to my word was the existential choice that made the rest of life meaningful. Once this was resolved, I was then interested in how we become moral and how character is formed.

During this same period of time I was introduced to the writings of Erik Erikson, one of the foremost developmental psychologists of the twentieth century, and to the work of Evagrius of Pontus (345-399), the original source of the "eight deadly thoughts." Together, these two individuals helped me understand the depths of our character and this hidden dimension of life. As I read *Childhood and Society*, Erikson's classic on the psychosocial development of humans, I began to understand the order and pattern of our own growth and development.[9] At the core of Erikson's thought is his identification and treatment of eight individual stages of development that require resolution of a competing commitment (trust versus mistrust, for example) in a social context.

During this same period, Allen introduced me to Evagrius of Pontus's eight deadly thoughts and their disorienting effect on our character. The unique contribution of Evagrius was his ability to look into the life of a leader and discern what would cause his or her demise. Of equal importance, however, was his willingness and ability to identify and illustrate how we can develop life-giving virtues that counteract these deadly thoughts and contribute to our success.

Together, Erikson's ideas and Allen's use of Evagrius demonstrate that at each stage of our development we face a challenge that is unique and must be resolved for us to successfully mature. The same is true of our development as leaders: just as our development as humans has a specific challenge at each stage, so our development as leaders faces a unique challenge at each stage. This specific challenge must be resolved if we are to continue to grow. Consider table 1.1, which identifies the vice and the virtue that correspond to each level of the leadership pyramid.

Table 1.1. Eight Vices and Virtues of the Leadership Pyramid

Eight Deadly Vices	Eight Life-Giving Virtues	Pyramid Level
1. Gluttony: an insatiable desire to consume or hoard because we fear there won't be enough—food, drink or even career opportunities.	1. Temperance: a recognition that we can exercise restraint in the short run because there will always be enough—food, drink and even additional career opportunities.	1. Character
2. Envy: resenting the gifts and abilities of others. (In Erikson's scheme, envy and anger are reversed.)	2. Contentment: Celebrating the gifts and abilities of others because we are content with our own gifts and abilities.	2. Competence
3. Greed: a boundless grasping, typically for money or fame, without respect for others.	3. Generosity: the capacity to self-limit in order to help those who are less fortunate than ourselves. It includes having the capacity to help others as well as the capacity to notice the needs of those around us.	3. Chemistry

4. Anger: "The most fierce passion is anger," Evagrius writes. "In fact, it is a boiling and stirring up of wrath against one who has given injury or offense. It leads to a preoccupation with the one with whom we are angry. It ruins our health—both physical and mental."[1]	4. Mildness: the ability to maintain our emotional and intellectual balance through self-restraint.	4. Culture
5. Pride: having an unwarranted and exaggerated sense of our own gifts and abilities.	5. Humility: the ability to see our gifts and abilities accurately in order to have an accurate view of the gifts and abilities of others.	5. Compatibility
6. Lust: having an egocentric belief that others exist strictly to satisfy our unbridled desires.	6. Fidelity: having the capacity to honor and respect others by cultivating an attitude of integrity, care and respect.	6. Convictions
7. Indifference: believing how we are currently investing our life does not matter or have any enduring value.	7. Perseverance: having a capacity to endure difficult circumstances without any hope of quick resolution because of a commitment to contribute to the greater good.	7. Connections
8. Melancholy: believing that both our current state and our entire existence do not matter.	8. Perspective: the ability to recognize that our contribution has mattered and release our life work to the next generation with confidence it will be acknowledged for its contribution.	8. Contribution

[1]Evagrius of Pontus, *The Praktikos & Chapters on Prayer,* trans. John Eudes Bamberger (Kalamazoo, Mich.: Cistercian, 1981), p. 18.

Harnessing these eight deadly thoughts requires the cultivation of the corresponding life-giving virtues. At each stage our character will develop appropriately if we work through each challenge successfully. In turn, our successful resolution at each level will establish a foundation of trust that makes our leadership effective.

Drucker emphasized the importance of character and trust, noting:

> The final requirement of effective leadership is to earn trust. To trust a leader, it is not necessary to like him. Nor is it necessary to agree with him. Trust is the conviction that the leader means what he says. Effective leadership—and again this is very old wisdom—is not based on being clever; it is based primarily on being consistent.[10]

We express this consistency, moreover, when we respond effectively to the leadership challenge that comes at each level of the pyramid. This challenge must be resolved for us to lead well. Although the whole chart pertains to the formation of character, we encounter a unique moral challenge at each stage of our leadership.

Thus, on the first level, where the primary focus is the development of our character, the vice is gluttony and the corresponding virtue is temperance. Gluttony is the insatiable desire to control and to consume by satisfying our fears and desires through gorging. We not only want to consume continuously, we want to ensure that we can do so. As a result, gluttony leads to a complete disorientation from the moral life. Although associated primarily with food, gluttony refers to any number of behaviors that reflect a loss of confidence and trust in the future and an unbridled need to control.

But how does this pertain to our leadership? As leaders, we often fear a decline in effectiveness, the loss of a leadership position or inadequacy. This deadly thought is manifested in compulsive overwork. We begin to feel that no amount of effort will be enough, and our compulsion causes an inability to trust: an inability to trust our personal capacities, the people responsible for our welfare and even the people we are responsible to lead. This absence of trust is often compounded by the return of memories of disheartening experiences from our past that sabotage our confidence in the goodness of others.

The virtue of temperance brings balance back to our life. Temperance helps us find our confidence in appropriate levels of contribution and hard work. We are able to exercise self-restraint at work because we learn to trust that our contribution matters. By developing this virtue, we learn to rely on others. Temperance is based on a capacity to trust that life will turn out okay. It also represents an ability to see the cyclical nature of life: that every downturn eventually has an upturn if we persevere with hope.[11]

Ten Essential Qualities That Reflect Our Character

The lost element of character formation is developing benchmarks that help us determine if we are making headway or are completely off-track. These measurements of progress are captured in the following ten qualities. The extent to which we express these qualities fundamentally reflects the health and vitality of our character and the level to which we are likely to achieve long-term success. A leader with well-formed character

1. leads from a foundation of integrity.

2. displays wisdom and judgment.

3. has the ability to absorb and undo the evil of others.

4. works with understanding and respect.

5. works for the greater good.

6. is temperate in all matters.

7. balances a confidence in his or her own ability with humility.

8. is calm, loyal, prudent and discerning.

9. hires well, communicates clearly and trusts.

10. balances a concern for the welfare of employees with the need to achieve positive results.[12]

First, the effective leader *leads from a foundation of integrity.* Webster defines integrity as "fidelity to moral principles, honesty, soundness, completeness." This means being true to our word and avoiding false appearances.

One of the most important realities leaders face is that their lives are always on display. People do not intend to be intrusive, but they often are. As public figures we can either resent intrusion or embrace it, since it never goes away. Once we've embraced this reality, we understand that everything we do has to be aboveboard and beyond reproach.

The effective leader also *displays wisdom and judgment* about the basic facets of running a successful business. This inspires the trust and confidence of our board, our work associates and our clients. The higher we go in a corporation, the more time we spend accomplishing our work through other people. Technical competence gets us the job, but relational competence helps us advance. All of us are hired for our abilities, but we advance in our positions because of our attitudes, behaviors and conduct.

I have worked in several settings where the difference in technical competence between certain individuals was very slim, but the difference in relational competence was large. In every case the person with higher levels of relational competence was given more responsibilities and wider influence than those without it.

Equally important, the effective leader *has the ability to absorb and undo the evil of others.* This requires maturity and is a real test of our character. Every organization I have ever served had ungracious associates and customers. Being able to make a gracious response to an ungracious person is a hallmark of character formation. Over time, an organization can develop dysfunctional interpersonal dynamics. Equally difficult, the leader also bears the brunt of attacks that occur between employees or are targeted at the organization. Both tasks require skill and insight.

Such ability is not natural to humans; rather, reflection and discipline equip a leader to discern the real problem and how best to respond. The effective leader also *works with understanding and respect* for each member of the organization. This virtue cannot be manufactured; instead, it arises from a fundamental disposition of integrity. One of the main manifestations of integrity is the willingness and ability to identify, develop and celebrate the gifts of those who work for you. To achieve the level of quality we need in our organization, we must be committed to gaining our employees' goodwill by giving them the opportunity to develop their capacities to the fullest. Often, it requires a level of confidence in our own gifts and abilities in order to develop the gifts and abilities of those we lead.

Drucker's emphasis on making our strengths effective and our weaknesses irrelevant had a great effect on Marcus Buckingham, the author of two classics on workplace satisfaction. In both *First, Break All the Rules* and *Now, Discover Your Strengths*, Buckingham emphasizes the importance of identifying and developing the unique gifts and abilities of everyone in our organizations. It dovetails beautifully with Jim Collins's emphasis in *Good to Great* on getting the right people on the bus and then getting them into the right seats.

To amplify this point, consider this legendary story of Sam Walton and his early days working for J. C. Penney. Sam was nearly fired because he was unable to fill out sales reports in a timely, accurate manner. Even though his sales exceeded every other person by a wide margin, this one weakness nearly cost him his job. Fortunately, a high-ranking supervisor intervened, recognizing that accuracy in reporting was secondary to results, and thus helped the company avoid a historic mistake.

I wonder, though, if this experience of being treated disrespectfully ultimately caused Walton to leave the company. So often, negative interaction on a persistent basis with one's direct supervisor is a key reason people choose to pursue a new position elsewhere.

Of course, the effective leader also *works for the greater good*, an important corollary to the previous emphasis on developing those who work in our organizations. Leaders today are tempted to use their current positions to promote themselves. Conversely, those who work for the greater good are not motivated by self-promotion; instead, they look out for the interests of the organization. One notable example is taken from the life of Red Poling, the retired chair and CEO of Ford Motor Company, and the featured mentor of chapter four.

Soon after Poling first joined our university board of trustees in Michigan, he was speaking at a business forum and was asked by one of our students what "moves" he had made to achieve such a prestigious position. His answer was classic: he responded that it had never been his goal to become CEO at Ford. In fact, he had initially retired from Ford when the board of directors asked him to run the company. His point in this illustration was to help the student understand that when we work for the greater good of our organization, the results speak for themselves and lead naturally to a promotion. This is a beautiful example of Drucker's principle that we do not plan a career, we manage it. And by managing our career, we take responsibility for our own development.

It is important for us to recognize that our most satisfying work will comprise efforts that serve purposes greater than ourselves. This is work for the greater good. Yet most of the messages our culture sends today are self-centered and self-focused. Hopefully, through character formation, we can recover an ability to sublimate our own interests for the greater good and strive for results that benefit our company.

The effective leader also is *temperate in all matters*. A leader who demonstrates moderation in all things, including moderation in response to renegade employees, does not overreact or bring unnecessary crises upon the company. This is often difficult to accomplish, but is so essential. Because every leader has opportunities to do both good and ill, necessary restraints must be established. These necessary restraints include policies, guidelines and strategic plans that define reality and help channel the priorities and decisions of the organization. Temperance also includes a spirit of toleration that keeps leaders from retaliating. Those who retaliate often gain a reputation for acting with contempt and disregard for people under their care.

At one time or another, we've all probably worked for a boss who acted like an "ambush predator," always waiting for the perfect moment to launch a surprise attack. I've had that experience. In one particular example, no matter how often we kept this person informed of our work, he or she would call surprise meetings and go on the attack. In one of my most memorable experiences, I was nearly two hours from our office when I was asked to return in order to handle a personnel matter that was not serious. This was not a crisis situation and there was no reason to make this demand other than to exert control over a subordinate. This experience didn't cause me to move on, but it did influence my decision when a new opportunity arose.

This is why it is so important that the effective leader is temperate when responding to employees. Temperance and mercy guide the effective leader to consider an associate's particular behavior in the broader perspective of his or her overall performance rather than immediately reacting with a rash response. Though an organization obviously cannot endure a tyrant, a sloth or an insubordinate, a leader who pauses long enough to determine whether an individual's behavior is an aberration or a normative pattern will be able to lead effectively. Maintaining our composure in all circumstances is critical.

Then, the effective leader must *balance confidence in his or her ability with humility*. In *Good to Great*, Collins notes that the most

effective leaders have low ego needs and find their greatest satisfaction in leading their organization to successful results. Being
confident in our ability but humble in our approach requires that
we learn to celebrate the gifts of those around us and to recognize
that our fortunes could change at any time.

In this regard, Drucker often commented on Avis, the rental car
company with the slogan "We try harder." What appealed to
Drucker was their knowledge that they were not number one, and
as a result they had to work harder and smarter in order to keep
their customers. The following lesson always focused on the necessity of assuming our competition is smarter, faster and better
capitalized than we are. Drucker also noted that the first and main
way companies get into trouble is by believing they have surpassed
any potential future problems.

Another critical ingredient is the need for the effective leader to
be calm, loyal, prudent and discerning. An excitable leader often
lacks proper restraint. Eventually, associates lose confidence in a
leader who cannot control his or her emotions, knowing at any
moment they could become the targets of an unprovoked attack.

In addition, effective leaders *hire well, communicate clearly and
trust the people they hire to achieve results.* Work associates do not
trust a micromanager. Micromanagement is a direct result of a
lack of trust, either in the people we have hired or in our ability to
communicate a compelling mission and vision for our organization. Such communication includes defining the measurements of
performance and the tactics and strategies needed to achieve desired results.

Trust is built on experience and perception. Over time, perception becomes almost more dominant then experience. A question-
able activity is accepted as legitimate when a person has earned
the right to receive "the benefit of the doubt." When trust erodes,
however, the same activity undermines our confidence in our associates. Prudence and discernment help us understand our busi-

ness as well as the deeper motive patterns of our colleagues. It helps us recognize that every employee is unique, and our management style needs to account for these differences.

One of my experiences of this principle occurred when I was a dean. As part of my responsibilities I supervised a high-performing individual who did not function effectively within conventional work hours. Initially, I was concerned about what it would mean for this individual to come and go at different hours and whether it would jeopardize our effectiveness as a team. Over time, however, I came to realize that this person was the highest performing individual in his area even though he followed a different rhythm in his life and work. This insight was a result of several conversations in which we were able to establish a relationship of trust. This mutual trust, in turn, helped me understand this individual's work patterns and shifted my focus from how he worked to what results he achieved. This shift in focus helped me avoid making a costly mistake.

Finally, the effective leader *balances a concern for the overall welfare of employees with the need to achieve positive results.* It is imperative that we meet the basic obligations of our company. A company cannot stay in business without meeting the needs and demands of its business. As Drucker often emphasized, the first responsibility of business is to meet the cost of capital in order to stay in business. Yet the companies that move from good to great are capable of long-term sustainable success because they balance the necessity of achieving long-term results with care of their people.

As I have attempted to demonstrate, character formation is progressive and is never finished. As we go through life, and our leadership responsibilities increase, our character will be tested at new and higher levels of intensity. To maintain consistency and grow in effectiveness requires that we establish a foundation of integrity that never wanes. This foundation is established by engaging in the disciplines of the moral life that can sustain us.[13]

Throughout this chapter I have attempted to identify the building blocks of character. We have considered the deadly thoughts that short circuit our effectiveness and the life-giving virtues that sustain us. We have also considered the unique qualities and disciplines that the effective leader must develop. These qualities and disciplines are both indicators of our maturity and an inventory of our need. The development of these qualities and disciplines is essential to our leadership.

Of course, to lead well we need to execute core competencies that develop over time. Our character forms the foundation of our leadership, but the threshold competencies that are built upon our character determine our success.

Principle 2

THE IMPORTANCE
OF COMPETENCE

Threshold Competencies and the
Essentials of Effective Leadership

An effective leader is not one who does things right;
It is one who does the right things. . . . Every managerial unit other than
top management is designed for one specific major task.
The one exception is top management. Its job is multidimensional.
There is no top-management task; there are only top-management tasks.

Peter Drucker

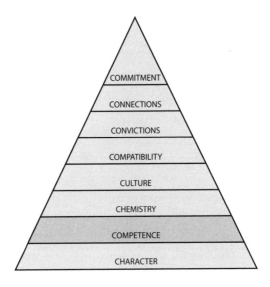

"Our goal for your education," began Drucker, "is to turn you from specialists into generalists." The context for this remark was his first lecture to our Management of People at Work class in the fall of 1990. "For example," he continued, "we want you to take enough accounting not so that you will become an accountant, but so that you will recognize when you are being embezzled." Then, with a twinkle in his eye, he added, "But if they're really good you won't be able to tell until it's too late anyway." His goal for our education was quite straightforward: teach us how to recognize the grand patterns and overarching themes into which all the discrete particulars of business could fit.

This first class was my introduction to his philosophy of management, which in turn was my introduction to his philosophy of education for the effective leader. I had been learning the roles and responsibilities of leadership, but the next two-and-a-half years would give me the framework to understand this work more completely.

We all need mentors, and we need them for our entire lives. Peter Drucker entered my life when I was ripe for the learning. I have often thought what a remarkable gift it was to study with him as I was entering adult responsibilities of leadership. To this day, I often find myself in situations where a point he made or a passage of his massive corpus comes back to me and gives me the right insight to address a specific challenge.

One of the great challenges for leaders is learning how to recognize patterns and connections. In fact, Drucker believed this is one of the great challenges in turning a specialist into a generalist. Drucker emphasized the importance of a liberal arts education, which he believed was the best training for learning how to synthesize discrete pieces of information into a meaningful whole. He amplified his philosophy by often stating that management is what tradition used to call a "liberal art": *liberal* because it deals with all the fundamentals of knowledge, *art* because it is concerned with practice and application.

My own educational background is in the tradition of the liberal arts. What I have found so helpful in Drucker's approach is his emphasis that all knowledge must be brought to bear on our challenges. Because we live and work in complex situations, we cannot know ahead of time all of the information and resources we will need to answer these challenges. Therefore, we need to develop a strong foundation in the liberal arts and then commit ourselves to lifelong learning so that we can continually expand our repertoire in order to generate new and innovative solutions to our problems.

Drucker believed that managers must be capable of drawing on all the knowledge of the academic disciplines, though they also must focus this knowledge on effectiveness and on results.[1] Drucker's management philosophy offers highly compelling arguments for the value of a liberal arts education in the training of society's leaders.

Drucker always stressed that leaders are made, not born.[2] The development of top management competencies requires an ability both to identify and execute key management functions and to develop of the leader whose growth is of such vital interest to the organization. Of key importance is developing a habit of effectiveness—that is, the capacity to get the right things done on a consistent basis.[3]

Elsewhere, Drucker defined the top management function: ensuring that every key activity and every key relation is covered. In other words, the plans for work must include assigning someone to do it. Top management tasks are those that are performed by the few individuals in every organization who are obligated to see the business as a whole.[4] They are responsible for establishing the purpose and mission of the organization. They are accountable for ensuring that work is productive and the worker is effective. Ultimately, they are tasked with seeing that social impacts and social responsibilities are fulfilled in such a way that they enhance rather than harm society.[5]

In his own trademark way Drucker summarizes the importance of the effective leader by noting,

> The rise of executive leadership has transformed the social and economic fabric of the developed world. The fundamental task of management is to make people capable of joint performance through common goals, common values, the right structure and the training and development they need to perform and respond to change.[6]

Drucker was not only ahead of his time, but he also defined his era. His recognition that the center of modern society is the "managed institution" helped give rise to the corporations that form the center of our modern economy.[7] His further emphasis that effective leadership is based on a very few essential principles helped a whole generation transcend the mechanistic horror of the modern factory to realize leadership is about human beings.

As Drucker notes, leadership deals with the integration of people in a common venture and is deeply embedded in an organization's tradition, history and culture. It reflects a commitment to common goals and shared values that are constituted by "simple, clear, unifying objectives based on a clear mission and vision."[8] In this way the effective leader guides the organization and helps each of its members to grow and develop as needs and opportunities change.

Effective leadership also requires regular and effective communication. Because people have different skills and abilities and are asked to do a variety of different tasks, effective communication is necessary if individuals are to understand how their contribution fits into the greater whole. Accountability, in turn, can only be built on shared communication that ensures personal responsibility. Ultimately, effective leadership is based on developing guiding paradigms and dependable principles.

Throughout his writing and teaching career, Drucker covered this familiar territory multiple times. In the process, he identified and then amplified the key competencies that constitute the effective leader. Beginning with *The Effective Executive,* Drucker identifies eight key qualities of the effective leader.[9] Later, while writing *Management: Tasks, Responsibilities, Practices,* Drucker amplified this original list by accenting two key tasks applied to five basic operations.[10] And still later, he would expand this list again when he offered twelve distinct practices that constitute the responsibilities of top management.[11] These writings, of course, fit into the broader context of the rise of executive leadership in the twentieth century.[12]

The Tasks of Leadership That Lead to Effectiveness

First and foremost is the contrast between effectiveness and efficiency. Drucker insisted we recognize that being mired in greater efficiencies often prevents an organization from thinking through whether it should be doing the work at all. As a result, great leaders must balance a commitment to efficiency with a relentless pursuit of effectiveness.

In my own experience, we have to do both. The top management team and the CEO must ensure both efficiency and effectiveness as they weigh the impact of both short-term results and long-term effectiveness on the company.

Drucker is relentless on the need for effectiveness. He often rehearsed his multiple lists with a precision that cut through our fuzzy thinking. "The manager's real work is a perpetual focus on effectiveness. This is accomplished in the five following ways":

- by developing a plan of action
- by determining a method of analysis
- by cultivating an understanding of the tools he or she needs

- by making decisions
- by committing to a course of action, and allocating resources so that the greatest opportunities can be realized[13]

Believing the purpose of an effective leader is the same across all industries, Drucker insists that we learn to ask the following questions in the same sequence in order to grasp the nature and context of our work.

First, what is the task? This is based on addressing the question, "What is our business, and is this what it should be?"

When we ask this question it raises a second, equally important question, *What are we doing currently that does not contribute to this task?* We are often tempted to ask how can we do something better when we should be asking whether it should be done at all. To answer this question adequately we have to establish clear objectives and goals based on our mission and vision.

Once we identify the answer to the second question, we can face a third: *What can we do to eliminate any activity that does not contribute to the fulfillment of our core task?*[14] This helps to establish the appropriate priorities that lead to our measurable results.

We then need to *define measurements of performance,* including the development of the metrics that lead to personal responsibility and self-control as well as an audit that measures objectives and goals against results. In this fashion we develop the capacity to identify and discontinue activities that are no longer serving their desired purpose or intent.[15]

This whole approach is based on a *theory of work and workers that value their distinct contribution.*[16] In what seemed highly controversial at the time, but now seems timely and relevant, Drucker suggested curbs on executive pay so as to reflect the true contribution top management makes to wealth creation in any given organization.

Drucker continued by emphasizing that *what we need today are* not *"how to do" tools, but "what to do" tools.* These tools would help us think about what should be done rather than only how to do better what is already being done. Of course, his favorite tool is the provocative question or the poignant observation. According to Drucker, the three primary areas where we need to think through what to do include *our assumptions about the external environment, our commitments regarding our central mission, and our performance of core competencies.*[17] Since the purpose of an organization is to get uncommon results from common individuals, it is imperative that we learn to *maximize strengths and neutralize weaknesses* by focusing on opportunities and people rather than problems and politics.[18]

Drucker pursues this line of thought more specifically by stating, "What makes executives effective is that they all follow the same eight practices."[19] These practices could be separated into three distinct areas of thought. "The first two practices," Drucker begins, "give them the knowledge they need; the next four help them convert this knowledge into effective action; and the last two ensure that the whole organization feels responsible and accountable"[20]—in other words, there are measurements of accountability that ensure results. These eight practices, the keys to our success, can be applied in any situation and lead us into the type of reflective thought so evident in Drucker's work.

Drucker's Eight Practices

1. Ask what needs to be done.
2. Focus not on what you like to do but on what is right for this organization.
3. Develop a bias for action and develop plans reflective of that bias.
4. Work to make effective decisions.
5. Communicate the appropriate amount of information at the appropriate level of transparency.
6. Maintain a focus on opportunities and innovations rather than problems.
7. Coordinate and run productive and effective meetings.
8. Build an effective team.

The first practice begins with a question: *What needs to be done?* The question is not What do I want to do? but What must we do to achieve results? The capacity to answer this question will determine our success. As leaders, we do not get to choose what we want to do each day. Each day must begin with asking what must get done.

One of Drucker's favorite examples was President Harry Truman. His respect for Truman was based on a number of factors, including his belief that Truman was one of the best-prepared domestic policy presidents in the history of our country. Unfortunately, Truman didn't inherit a country mired in domestic turmoil; he inherited a country on the brink of an international crisis. As a result, Truman began spending long hours every Saturday with foreign policy experts in order to develop his capacities to make discerning judgments on foreign affairs, an area in which he was initially ill-prepared to lead when he assumed office. This preparation proved invaluable when the Korean crisis escalated into war and he had to lead a weary nation back into combat.

This illustration lies at the heart of Drucker's first question (in three parts): Are we doing the things that need to be done that will fundamentally advance our organization? Are we doing those activities that only we can do and that will add value to our company? What do we need to stop doing so that we can attend to the items that will matter most for our organization's future?

As the president of a national liberal arts college, it is easy for me to get drawn into activities and experiences that will not advance our college. They are good activities and at some level even meaningful, but my entire calendar can get overrun with items that have little to do with the two or three core activities that I need to be doing to fundamentally advance our college. Because of Drucker's emphasis on the first practice, I often find myself stopping to ask, How will this activity fundamentally advance Westmont College? I don't always get the answer right, and not every activity ends up having the result I anticipate, but answering this question consistently has helped to refine my use of time and to maintain my focus.

Drucker's second question tests the capacity of the effective leader to sublimate his or her own ego needs in order to serve the greater good of the organization. He asks, *What is right for this enterprise?* This can only be established by determining the specific purpose and mission of our organization, including identifying our strengths and neutralizing our weaknesses. Over time, organizations develop a DNA that makes them exceptionally good at some things but not suited for everything.

In 2007, my family moved from Spring Arbor to Westmont. During the interview process I was asked if I was going to introduce the same types of graduate and undergraduate programs at Westmont that had worked so effectively at Spring Arbor. Clearly, the question was born from the concern that I might shift Westmont's core competency to something that didn't really fit its purpose and mission.

Yet, this specific question masked a larger question we should all carry: What are the opportunities for innovation that we can pursue at an institution? In my own evaluation of Westmont, I had concluded not only that the graduate and undergraduate programs we had developed at Spring Arbor did not fit Westmont, but also that Westmont did not have the culture or the internal resources to pursue these strategies effectively. What is true of Westmont is that we have tremendous strengths in other areas, and we need to leverage these strengths rather than try to replicate strategies based on the strengths of another institution.

Third, *the effective leader develops action plans.* Drucker emphasized that leaders must have a bias for action without throwing him- or herself at every problem or opportunity. Effective leaders need to make plans and follow them, first by determining the desired outcomes and then by evaluating these stated outcomes against real results. We also need to ensure our commitment to effectiveness by managing our time in relationship to these action plans. Successful time management can only be achieved when we first establish a clear set of plans and then tie our goals directly to their accomplishment.

In order to ensure that all the members of our executive team are on the same page each year, we start with an executive team retreat in the summer. The goal of the retreat is twofold: first, to introduce and discuss my goals for the upcoming year, and, second, to coordinate the goals of each vice president with our overarching goals as an organization. Because we are on an academic calendar for programming and a fiscal year for finances, our fiscal year officially begins on July 1. Our program year, however, doesn't start until mid-August. As a result, I always take my vacation in July and ask my vice presidents to complete their vacations by August 1. This gives us ten to twelve days back in the office to finish developing our plans before we engage in our two-day retreat. At the retreat each vice president presents his or her goals, and then we integrate the specific work of each area of the college into a meaningful whole. Later, at our fall board meeting, we present our goals to the board of trustees' planning committee, inviting their interaction and feedback. In this way we develop both a strong sense of corporate commitment and a significant level of personal accountability. In addition, this fall meeting provides a blueprint for the upcoming year and a process for making the essential decisions we will face.

Fourth, *an effective leader makes effective decisions.* Decisions are choices between alternative courses of action. Such choices are seldom made with complete clarity or confidence. More often than not the circumstances are ambiguous, and we make decisions that we believe to be "directionally correct." Because decisions dictate direction, we need to think through the decision-making process, and once we have made a decision, ensure that it is carried out. In keeping with this process, Drucker's template for effective decision-making includes six essential characteristics.[21]

The temptation, however, is to make decisions and then move on, assuming others will carry them out with the same burden of concern that we held when we made the decision. In reality, the adage that we must "inspect what we expect" lays the ground rules for being sure our decisions are successfully implemented.[22]

We have to apply the same rigor we use in general decision making to the specific challenge of *hiring decisions*. The people decisions we make fundamentally determine the trajectory and long-term effectiveness and success of our organization. This is why these decisions are so crucial. In order to ensure our success we need to be systematic in our approach. Think through the assignment. Consider several potentially qualified people. Narrow the field to two or three final candidates. Discuss the final candidate or candidates with people who have worked with them directly. Determine during the interview if the person offered the appointment is willing to accept. It is the fundamental responsibility of the effective leader to ensure the quality and training of the people hired because the strength and capacity of the organization relies on it. With few exceptions, organizations rarely rise above their talent level.[23]

Of course, there is also an issue of *timing and execution*.[24] Does the decision, whether program or personnel, need to be made immediately, before the end of the day, or before the end of the week? Or is there an imprecise deadline that lies in the future?

Finally, who will do the work? Unless a decision is followed by the assignment of responsibility, the decision will not be fulfilled.

Drucker's point is that unless a plan focuses the specific activities that comprise our work, it is just a plan and is not focused on results. Therefore, every decision must have the name of the person accountable for its implementation, the deadline for when it must be finished, the list of people who are influenced by the decision and therefore have to know about it, and the people who have no responsibility to see it fulfilled but must know the decision has been made, such as the board of directors and other relevant constituencies.[25]

Fifth, *the effective leader takes responsibility for communicating the appropriate amount of information at the appropriate level of transparency.* To be effective we need to communicate both our plans of action and the information we need in order to make effective decisions. In this way we establish that communication is a two-way process of understanding both what needs to be communicated (information) and how it should be communicated (context) for the greatest level of effectiveness. As a result, we must learn to communicate the right information at the right time, in the right way, for the right reason.

Different organizations have different communication needs and expectations. Some want a great deal of detail while others only want high-level information. Determining the pace, style and content of our communication is as important as determining the level of communication for each of our various constituencies. At Westmont, within our strategic planning process, we work to determine what needs to be communicated and at what level of transparency. Having the conversation has enhanced our understanding and execution of appropriate levels of communication.

Sixth, *effective leaders focus on opportunities and innovations rather than on problems.* Problem solving is necessary and must be done in order to prevent damage; however, our focus must be on opportunities and innovations where we produce results that extend the reach and influence of our organization. A key to being opportunity-focused is to have our best people working on our biggest opportunities.

To capture opportunities, Drucker insisted on innovation. In fact, he was especially interested in what his father's friend Joseph Schumpeter had termed "creative destruction," the practice of discontinuing certain activities in order to start new ones. To articulate and embrace this practice is to embrace a discipline of innovation throughout the organization. To create this culture of innovation and entrepreneurship, however, the effective leader must do the following. First, exhibit a relentless commitment to innovate and expand, continually scanning the industry for new trends and opportunities. Second, utilize sound financial principles in order to plan cash flow and capital needs in such a way that what is a cash cow today can feed the stars of tomorrow.[26] Third, build a top management team for the new venture long before the new venture actually needs one and long before it can actually afford one. Finally, the effective leader must determine what role he or she should assume within the new venture that will lead to the greatest likelihood of success.[27]

Seventh, *an effective leader runs productive meetings by determining in advance what the purpose of each meeting will be.* The values of the organization are reflected in the agenda of each meeting. Meetings also reflect the level of communication and input necessary for decisions to be fully integrated throughout the organization.

One of the greatest topics of complaint in any organization is the role and value of meetings, and the complaints aren't always about having too many meetings. I have been in some organizations where individuals complained that they didn't meet often enough. As a result, it is important to recognize that meetings have a variety of purposes, including social, personal and organizational purposes that go beyond the business of the agenda.

Thus, when we meet as an executive team for Westmont College, we always include area updates and points of personal concern. This routine reflects the priority we place on people in our organization and gives each of the vice presidents the opportunity to present information not directly tied to a decision. Then, to help us keep the meetings productive, we determine a start time and a finish time for each item, as well as determining before we start whether each item on the agenda is an information item, a discussion item or an action item. By thinking through the agenda before the meeting ever begins, we are able to stay on track with our action plans for the year and make adjustments when necessary. Figure 2.1 is an example of how we organize our agendas.

Title of Meeting

Attendees:

Invited guests (if any)

Time	Topic/Item	Person Responsible	Information/Discussion/Action

Figure 2.1. Typical Westmont College agenda

I have also discovered that maintaining a rolling tally of action items reminds me what has been accomplished and what still needs our attention.

Eighth, *an effective leader builds an effective team, through which the broader goals and objectives of the organization are achieved.* There are a variety of philosophies on how to build a team—every industry has its own pace and expectation. In fast-paced industries, it is critical that the leader establishes his or her team quickly and then begins work immediately. This often leads to high turnover when leadership changes.[28]

My industry, higher education, carries both an expectation and a priority of stability. As a result, I believe it is important to blend top management teams, combining an influx of trusted and effective colleagues from previous organizations with high-performing senior managers that are inherited. This strategy has proven highly effective each time I have come to a new assignment. The key, of course, is to be sure to fill each role with highly competent, well-performing people.

The one reality we have to accept is that the vice presidents we inherit often take longer to understand and embrace our vision and priorities than the ones we hire. This distinction is not always the case, but so often the vice presidents we inherit are making contributions that we tend to undervalue. There are a number of reasons for this tendency, but the most obvious is our natural orientation to staff our direct reports with people whose performance capacity we already know and respect. Of course, a tendency that can ruin teams and undermine effectiveness is if the vice presidents we inherit feel a spoken or unspoken responsibility to preserve the past and become resistant or obstructionist in the forward thrust of a new administration. We have to pay attention to both possibilities and make sure the team is focused on effectiveness and success.

Of course, these dynamics are true of teams at all levels of the organization. Everyone in the organization needs to feel that he or she has opportunities to grow and develop. This includes growing and developing beyond current assignments.

These eight practices were later amplified by Drucker's idea that the effective leader must integrate every individual into the greater whole. The CEO, in partnership with his or her executive team, is responsible for seeing that this integrative work occurs and must make it a priority since it never occurs automatically.[29]

Equally important to balancing the competing commitments and personalities within an organization is the need to harmonize the demands of immediate challenges with long-range needs and plans.[30] The effective leader then must set objectives in eight key areas (marketing, innovation, human resources, financial resources, physical resources, productivity, social responsibility and profit requirements), organizing the work and activities of the organization around these areas, and establishing appropriate benchmarks and measures. We are also responsible for cultivating the strengths of our work associates and developing our people.[31] This is "management by objectives" (MBO).[32] Ultimately, we need to recognize the breadth of our work and responsibility.[33] We must seek to understand our work and be open to refining it as new circumstances require such adjustments.[34]

Striving for Effectiveness

As a result, we need to remember that a key duty of the effective leader is to strive for the best possible economic results from the resources currently available.[35] Everything else flows from creating financial margins. Thus, a chief component of a CEO's work is to direct the resources and efforts of the business toward opportunities that are missionally sensitive and economically sound. Unfortunately, in almost all organizations the resources of time, attention and money are spent on problems rather than opportunities. How can we think through our work in order to turn this tendency around?

Because we often confuse effectiveness and efficiency, one of our greatest challenges is that almost all of our activity is consumed by trying to do things more efficiently rather than stopping to ask whether or not they should be done at all. To reverse this tendency, Drucker devised five probing questions to help us get focused on results rather than just activities.[36]

To answer these questions sufficiently we first have to determine how we can focus the greatest amount of our efforts on the smallest number of products, services and customers that stand to produce the greatest results. We must stop and consider where our greatest opportunities lie. What are the products or services, and who are the customers whose even more significant participation would lead to better results?

The same holds true for motivating our staff. The effective leader needs to focus his or her greatest efforts on the smallest number who will yield the largest results. We often believe that we need to treat everyone equally. While this is true in terms of fairness, this often disrupts our even greater need to pay attention to the few people who with 2 percent more time and resources would yield 20 percent more results. Consider: Who are these individuals in the organization, and what am I doing to motivate them?

Likewise, the effective leader must insert the appropriate level of cost controls in order to exert a significant impact on overall results. In this way we are able to allocate the necessary resources to those activities that provide the greatest opportunities for success.[37]

Unfortunately, most organizations operate with little regard for these principles and often operate in direct opposition to them. In order to develop our capacity to ask the right questions and exercise the right discipline in each of these areas, we need to follow three key steps. First, we need to analyze our situation in order to ascertain the facts, including what our current costs are and what our future opportunities will cost. Next, we need to evaluate what potential contributions could be made by different activities. Finally, we need to determine what our most significant cost centers are and whether or not the results justify our current priorities.

Then the effective leader needs to evaluate his or her allocation of all resources, including human resources, and determine whether they are achieving what they hoped they would. This process is straightforward. Begin with evaluating how resources are currently allocated to product or program lines, staff support activities and existing cost centers. Then consider how resources should be allocated in the future. Finally, determine what steps will be necessary to get from where we are currently investing our resources to where we need to invest our resources.

One of the tools I have developed to help me do this is a simple matrix to evaluate our personnel and program budgets. I have each vice president categorize his or her people and programs in one of two categories. The two categories for individuals or programs are "front counter" and "back room"; in other words, does the person or program interact directly with our highest priorities or does it serve a support role that is unseen? The second step is to have the vice presidents categorize their people and programs into one of four quadrants (see fig. 2.2).

3. Nonessential but effective	1. Essential and effective
4. Nonessential and ineffective	2. Essential but ineffective

Figure 2.2. Four quadrants of people and programs

This process helps guide our decision making. Of course, our goal is to keep the people and programs in quadrant one, and to take the resources in quadrant three and apply them to the opportunities in quadrant two. Any person or any program placed in quadrant four makes the decision to discontinue the person or program obvious.

The final step is the most difficult: deciding which products, costs and activities have to be curtailed or discarded altogether. This step means deploying Schumpeter's principle of creative destruction. The areas that fail to bring opportunities and results today will stymie the organization tomorrow.[38]

These core competencies form a lens through which effective leaders see their work and fulfill their responsibilities.

These responsibilities are never carried on our own. Even effective leaders continually work with a management team whose coordination and cooperation play a critical role in the long-term effectiveness of the company. Learning how to build a management team and learning how to work effectively within a management team are essential behaviors for our success.

The Quest for Character: Envy Versus Happiness
The character challenge at this level is envy. Envy awakens when

we feel inadequate about our own gifts and abilities and begin to resent the gifts and abilities of others. Envy is motivated by fears about losing our place. *What if someone else has better gifts than I do? Will I still be able to accomplish my own dreams and ambitions?* Envy ultimately prevents us from accepting our own gifts and abilities and from assuming a legitimate role in the social networks and organizations where we can find the greatest meaning. The strongest of the deadly thoughts, envy has the capacity to ruin us by not allowing us to embrace others.

The deeper and even more destructive side of envy is the desire to prevent another person from expressing his or her gifts and abilities altogether. This goes beyond just wanting to possess another's gift or ability: it includes wanting to deny the person the exercise and expression of his or her own gift. At its most extreme, envy reflects the desire to sabotage or destroy another person.

The corresponding virtue that breaks the power of envy is happiness or blessedness. Happiness (blessedness) is the internal capacity to celebrate the gifts and abilities of others. It is born of a recognition and acceptance that we have gifts too. It also recognizes that gifts and abilities differ and that everyone needs to find his or her rightful place in the forward thrust of the organization. Happiness arises from a celebration of mutual contribution, the contributions that we can make as well as those made by others with gifts and abilities that differ from our own.

Principle 3

THE ADVANTAGE
OF TEAM CHEMISTRY

The Role of the CEO and the Top Management Team in Creating a Climate of Effectiveness and Success

*Top management work is work for a team rather than for one man.
The basic specifications require a CEO to assign responsibilities
to a top-management team based on the fit of these responsibilities with
the personalities, qualifications, and temperaments of the members.*

Peter Drucker

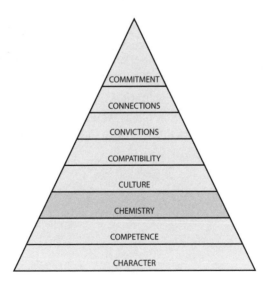

For the past twenty-six years I have been a part of various management teams, first as a mid-level manager and then for the past twelve years as a college and university president. My first experience with a multifunctional team felt like being on a track team in which each did his or her own work, added up the total score at the end of the day, and then combined scores, which defined our contribution. Although we coordinated our work and planned budgets and programs cooperatively, the results in one area were not necessarily coordinated with the results in any other area.

Then, in 1992, I entered higher education. For the first six years I was a mid-level manager with responsibilities for key programs and a full teaching load as a professor. I had weekly contact with my dean, monthly contact with our provost and regular contact with our president. The university was experiencing a major growth spurt, and it was an exciting time to be a part of entrepreneurial ventures that were achieving impressive results.[1] During that time I became a dean, which further accelerated my own development as a leader.

Our university president was an able administrator and an academic entrepreneur. He had completed his Ph.D. at Notre Dame University in South Bend, Indiana, and combined a strong commitment to academic quality with market sensitivities that were growth-oriented. He set the course and direction for the university, which continues to flourish following strategies and plans established during his presidency. During the eight years I was with him, he mentored me and provided insight into his thinking and decision making as a leader. It was enormously helpful and opened my mind to the possibility of providing executive leadership myself.

What I have learned through these experiences is that a good team always outperforms a group of strong but independent individuals. In other words, the whole is truly greater than the sum of the parts. I also came to realize the importance of teams at every level of the organization. When I was a department chair, our particular school within the university was responsible for performing at a level that enhanced rather than diminished the university. We relied on senior management to set the direction of the university, but executing that direction in our particular area depended on our capacity as an operating team.[2]

My larger point: a leader has to build an executive team that reflects both the priorities and the demands facing the organization. Much of the work of an executive team will be conventional, but every leadership position includes challenges unique to each situation that require innovation and will spur the leader to configure the team in the way most likely to generate success.[3]

In building my first executive team while at Spring Arbor, I focused on immediate challenges. In its financial circumstances the university needed a highly competent financial manager. Its academic programs, although solid, were not exhibiting a forward thrust that a school like Spring Arbor needed and deserved. Much of the political turmoil within the organization was a direct result of relinquishing too much power to a few senior executives who exceeded the scope and boundary of their job specifications. The result was a political culture that stymied confidence and clear progress toward set goals. By year three of my presidency the executive team was established and we engaged in what would become a five-year run with a significant and positive effect on Spring Arbor University.

Later, when building our executive team at Westmont, I have faced similar challenges to those of Spring Arbor but also some real differences. For instance, Westmont's culture is very different than Spring Arbor's. And the differences are much more than cosmetic ones. In fact, contrasts exist on almost every level, contrasts between sense of mission and purpose, between student profiles, even between the way each institution interfaces with the local community. Such cultural and institutional differences will and must influence us as leaders.

Nevertheless, the principles remained the same even though my second team faced an entirely different series of issues. Still, an effective leader needs to have the freedom to develop the team that he or she is most confident will fulfill the mission of the institution. Necessary constituencies have to be consulted along the way, and in some cases these constituencies must play a fundamental role in the selection process (e.g., the faculty's role in hiring a provost), but the president has to have confidence in the team that is assembled to do the work.

In addition, the team members must be individuals of high capacity and commitment. Due to highly demanding work schedules, these members must perform without needing daily guidance. This team dynamic is only possible if we maintain a team culture based on the four following guidelines and expectations: bad news first, full disclosure, no surprises, and be loyal to the work of the team or leave. This last responsibility is not a call to blind loyalty, but a recognition that robust disagreement must happen behind closed doors. We must have team discipline to defend one another and to defend the decisions we make together. If we don't, when the team's decisions enter the public arena and are openly questioned, we will undermine the trust and confidence we need in one another. This trust includes that of the chief executive. In fact, one of the most destructive patterns that can develop in an executive team is when the senior executive implies that although particular decisions were made, he or she didn't agree with them.

In both institutions the development of the executive team has been like playing a game of chess in which different pieces are being moved on the board as other pieces are removed altogether. As such, executive leadership requires thinking several moves ahead in anticipation of other challenges. In each institutional setting the need to blend continuing members with new members has been a key ingredient to achieving effectiveness as a team. We need an able mix of outsiders (who can help move the organization forward) balanced by insiders (who can preserve a sense of institutional continuity). We need people we can trust. We need to hire competent people who can work from general guidelines and not burden us with a need for constant supervision or correction throughout the day. Ultimately, we need a team who can do the work.

The purpose in sharing these scenarios is that in each situation the quality of the executive team fundamentally determined the capacity of these two institutions. In fact, in both assignments the opportunity to shape the executive team has enabled me to address unique challenges in highly effective ways.

Top Management Teams

Peter Drucker's treatment of top management teams is economical, to say the least, but what he had to say was of the utmost importance. He recognized their significance as well as the reliance of entire companies on the success or failure of senior leadership. "Top management work is work for a team rather than for one man."[4] He elaborated by specifying that a well-functioning team must have a capacity to understand and execute top-management tasks. He also insisted that every top-management task must not only be clearly understood but also specifically assigned to someone who has direct and full responsibility for it. This assignment of responsibilities must reflect an understanding of the fit with the personalities, qualifications and temperaments of the members of the team. Ultimately, to embrace our responsibilities fully as an executive team requires that we stop operating at other levels of the institution.[5]

Drucker went on to emphasize that the top-management team has to set the pace for effectiveness throughout the entire organization. This emphasis motivated him to refine the work of top management further. He incorporated guiding polices, insisting, for example, that no member will make a decision in an area where he or she does not carry primary responsibility. He amplified the importance of the team having a leader/coach. Drucker also stressed the importance of systematic and intensive communication among a team's members. Ultimately, team members need to know each other's functions and potential contributions. Drucker's one drawback in this arena is his deemphasis of the need for rapport, empathy and interpersonal relations among the members. Still, he did underscore the importance of mutual understanding of others' jobs and common understanding of the essential tasks.[6]

One of my all-time favorite leaders and certainly one of my favorite university presidents is Dr. Steve Sample, president emeritus of the University of Southern California. I met Dr. Sample shortly after I became president of Spring Arbor in 2000. I was serving on a board with Dallas Willard, a noted author and a great philosopher who teaches at USC. During one of our breaks Willard said to me, "You know, if you ever get a chance to meet my president, he's about the best I've ever seen." This struck me as high praise coming from Willard, both because of his own personal stature and also because you almost never hear a faculty member speak this way about his or her president!

Here is what surprised and pleased me. When I was preparing to come to Southern California in the winter of 2001, I called Dr. Sample's office to see if I could get even ten minutes with him. His assistant took the call, and we had a nice conversation. I told her of my friendship with Dallas Willard, whom she knew, and when I asked for an appointment with Sample, she shared something that stunned me: he would be happy to meet with me, but he almost never gets asked. I could hardly believe my good fortune; one of the finest presidents in the history of higher education was available for a conversation with a young president. Our initial conversation was by phone, but it started a friendship that continues to this day.

Steve Sample is a remarkable leader. He combines a brilliant intellect with a deft touch in human relations. Trained as an electrical engineer, he destroys every stereotype of the introverted nerd unable to win a date. He is charming, funny and a joy to be with. I leave every encounter with Sample feeling changed and inspired.

I have never worked for Sample, but he has allowed me to see him in action on different occasions, and these occasions have been impressive. He outlined his approach to leadership in a provocative volume titled *The Contrarian's Guide to Leadership.*[7] Despite his advice to read only books that are at least four hundred years old, his book is well worth the effort and rewards even a casual reading.

Of all the topics his book engages, his treatment of how to hire, build and motivate a team is the most compelling. It begins with his basic principle, "Work for those who work for you." The premise is clear: once you have settled on your team, do everything you can to make them succeed because your success as a leader will be fundamentally tied to their successes as your "chief lieutenants."[8]

Of course, to have a great leadership team requires that we hire great individuals into every senior-level position. This is where Sample deploys his 99 percent rule.[9] In sum, the 99 percent rule states that if leaders hire a person who has 99 percent of their ability and working capacity, they will get a person who functions at a 98 percent capacity. If they, in turn, hire a person who is functioning at 98 percent of his or her capacity, then at the next level down leaders will get a 96 percent person. And if this third person hires a fourth person who functions at 96 percent of his or her capacity, that combination will result in a 92 percent person. Sample's point is that we can be four levels deep in the organization and still have solid A-grade performances at all levels.

By contrast, if a leader begins by hiring a person who is only 90 percent of him- or herself, then the leader will get a person who elicits an 81 percent total capacity. If he or she, in turn, hires a person who functions at 81 percent capacity, that combination will result in a person who has 66 percent total capacity. And if this third-level employee hires a person who functions at 66 percent of his or her capacity, that combination will result in a person of 43 percent capacity. Sample's point is quite obvious: hiring people of lower capacity, even 90 percent versus 99 percent, quickly lowers the overall capacity of the organization. As a result, Sample believes that the leader must hire the best available person into every position, and that doing so fundamentally determines the trajectory of the organization. He also encourages those advertising positions not to obsess about crafting a perfect job description. In every case, Sample advises, great people are more important than great job descriptions.

Sample is also attentive to the dynamic interplay between those who report directly to us as well as the importance of good working relationships. I think Sample is absolutely right. Recent books featuring warring officers (e.g., the depiction of Lincoln's cabinet in *Team of Rivals*) suggest an approach to executive interaction that is difficult to sustain and often undesirable. Even though a bestselling book like *Team of Rivals* may profile and even applaud executive contention, such success should not distract us from the unique circumstances of the team (the Civil War) and its unique timeline (Lincoln's team was together less than four years). A team fueled by rivalry may be a great model for crisis management, but it is hard to find evidence that such teams are sustainable over time.

But how do we get the senior executives on our leadership team to like each other? Those who report to us behave much better when they have unfettered access to the chief executive. They also behave better when their annual evaluations are conducted by the chief executive rather than farmed out to a consulting firm with no ongoing relationship and no ongoing contact with the culture and needs of the organization. Delegating these key responsibilities to someone else breeds distrust, and distrust eventually destroys a team.

Unfettered access to us occurs in two ways. First, by scheduling regular one-on-one meetings we allow predictable, structured interaction to occur. Second, we have to remain available to them, anytime, anywhere. The mere thought of knowing we are available will almost certainly give our executive team the peace of mind to do their work effectively.

Sample also insists that just as good news must be conveyed directly, so must bad news. In other words, we should take personal responsibility for hiring, evaluating, promoting and firing our direct reports. This requires regular and annual interaction regarding their achievements, shortcomings and contributions to the organization. Ultimately, it works best if we can help a person who needs to leave our team do so of his or her own accord after hearing our evaluation.

Finally, every leader knows that they live and die by their direct reports. As Sample notes, choosing these people and then doing everything in our power to motivate and equip them will be one of the most significant contributions we make both to our own success and that of the organization.[10]

Building Great Teams and Fostering Teamwork

The responsibility of the leader is to build an effective executive team. This executive team is responsible for helping fulfill the strategic mission of the organization. In building a great executive team, an effective leader demonstrates his or her commitment to maximizing the strengths of others for the greater good of the organization. In this way the leader creates an institutional value system that guides the entire organization.

By developing a great executive team, the effective leader also demonstrates a commitment to a values-based organization that is dedicated to the welfare of its people. This values-based orientation focuses on maximizing their potential. It demonstrates an inherent value and respect for individual gifts and differences that strengthens the organization. Ultimately, it allows individuals to work in their areas of greatest strength and thereby discover fulfillment through their work.

In 2002, the Gallup Organization conducted an extensive study on the Toyota Motor Corporation and its legendary commitment to building great teams. The discoveries that were eventually formulated into the StrengthsFinder program included a commitment to obtaining and implementing ideas from all their associates,[11] the cultivation of a culture of respect by creating an expectation that motivated workers should offer meaningful contributions, and a focus on identifying and utilizing each member's unique personal strengths for the greater good of the company.[12] Through this program Toyota developed a series of 180-paired statements that helped individuals understand where they could be most effective. This tool encouraged individuals and teams to focus on building their strengths rather than trying to minimize their weaknesses.

Toyota's focus that led to StrengthsFinder helped create a culture that reinforced another significant value: using the collective decision-making skills of the team members rather than maintaining a hierarchical command-and-control atmosphere, which is typical of manufacturing. This value encouraged a learning environment that created cross-training among employees. It strengthened morale. It contributed to an overall sense of achievement. It helped create a positive atmosphere in which peer pressure motivated the team as a whole. Eventually, this led to the development of a "great managers" program, a key tool in developing and distributing this philosophy throughout the company. Ultimately, the real test was that this commitment improved quality and expanded productivity.

The principles from this study that I have found most effective include the necessity of understanding the strengths of my work associates, the importance of determining the right size of my team in order to accomplish my work, and the strength that comes from developing a participative style of decision making.

A corollary to StrengthsFinder is the work of Daniel Goleman and especially his focus on "working with emotional intelligence."[13] This landmark study identifies thirteen personal and twelve social qualities that make a person effective. He is especially helpful in his general philosophy as well as its specific application to the development of collaboration, teams and group IQ.[14]

Goleman's work originated as he was trying to determine why the people with the highest IQ seldom if ever achieve the greatest success. Through the years his multiple studies and projects have identified twenty-five competencies that he divides into two distinct levels and five specific categories. In level one, personal competence, he places self-awareness, self-regulation and motivation. In level two, social competence, he places empathy and social skills. Then, within each category he lists three or four specific qualities.

Goleman's list includes more than can be absorbed easily or quickly, but I have been working with his material for ten years and have found it to be extremely effective at helping alert leaders to what they both should and should not be doing. His work rewards a careful reading since his research helps leaders understand and pursue the necessary qualities that produce effectiveness.[15]

Goleman's work illustrates the importance of understanding how our individual qualities determine our level of effectiveness in a broader social context. In balancing our personal and social qualities, we come to realize the way the goals and objectives of the team become equally important to the achievement of our own goals and objectives. By building personal bonds with other employees, we help create the sort of informal networks that we need for effectiveness and success. It also gives us the opportunity to develop friendships at work that make our job meaningful and enjoyable. In building a reservoir of goodwill, we develop the capacity to collaborate and cooperate with others while achieving the shared goals of the organization.

Achieving the shared goals of the organization requires a level of trust and support that is only possible when meaningful relationships are present. These relationships, in turn, allow a cooperative spirit to develop that prevents sabotage and makes effectiveness possible. Although the importance of relational equity in organizations is sometimes downplayed, there is no doubt that today's workers want to find meaning and purpose through their work, including meaning and purpose through their relationships at work.

Such meaning is acquired when the team exemplifies qualities of respect, helpfulness and cooperation. There has to be a level of confidence in each other's abilities and a level of respect that transcends difference. And concern for all members of the team has to be demonstrated. Demonstrating concern entails communicating openly and utilizing appropriate levels of confrontation when team members make mistakes; it also entails maintaining the overall commitment of the team to group accomplishment.

This commitment is often reinforced by what we honor and celebrate as a team. The adage that *what a culture honors, it produces* is true for organizations. Celebrations by the team should recognize individual contributions while framing these contributions by celebrating the achievements of the whole. Emphasizing team versus individual accomplishments demonstrates that we value the team. In this way, a reward structure should reinforce the values of the team and help strengthen the sense of common purpose that is needed throughout the organization.

Managing an Executive Team and Leading an Organization

In managing my executive team I begin with key input from each vice president and then work toward a common commitment distilled in an executive team covenant. Both at Spring Arbor and Westmont we have used the following guidelines at the start of each year to focus our interaction.

- Prepare an annual plan for what you intend to achieve in the upcoming year. Think through your most significant assignments. How are these reflected in your personal goals and our corporate goals as an institution?

- As you reflect on this past year, prepare a brief review, one to two pages, of how you feel you did relative to your annual plan.

- Prepare a brief statement of your ongoing personal philosophy of leadership and how it has grown or changed since last year.

- What plans do you have for continuing education and professional development this year?

- What are the areas we need to work on together both for the success of the institution and for your personal contribution to this success?

- Please offer your thoughts on how our team is functioning at the executive-team level and your perspective on the distribution of workload and responsibilities.

- What ideas or experiences would you like to see us incorporate into our executive-team leadership retreats in the future?

- What are your thoughts on our competitors? Who are they, where are they eclipsing us, where are we eclipsing them, and what information do you feel we need to discuss that would help us face our competitive mix better?

- What are key projects that you believe would fundamentally advance the mission of our institution?

- What contribution from me do you require in order to make your own contribution to our institution more meaningful and effective?

Of course, each leader should make this list unique to his or her personality and organization. The key is to go through the discipline of the exercise. This exercise establishes a way for an executive team to discuss their joint work as a team. This sets the stage for one-on-one conversations with each of my vice presidents, which is instrumental in strengthening our leadership and effectiveness.

Then, every executive team retreat ends with a review of our executive team covenant and our willingness to abide together by its public commitments.[16] Here is the latest iteration of our executive team covenant, written collaboratively and then reviewed each year:

> We, the executive team of Westmont College, commit to the following as a means for creating and maintaining strong relationships within the team, and for achieving the strategic goals of the college.
>
> 1. Full disclosure, no surprises, and bad news first. To establish a foundation of trust, we agree to be vulnerable within the group, to be open and genuine regarding our mistakes and weaknesses, with the knowledge that the group will be protective of the information that has been shared and of the person that has shared it. We agree to give each other the benefit of the doubt in circumstances where issues have been raised about another member's area of responsibility, allowing that member an opportunity to review the situation and respond to the group.
>
> 2. We agree to avoid veiled discussions and guarded comments, and instead, we will engage in genuine and direct

conversation regarding the strategies and tactics for advancing Westmont College.

3. First and primary responsibility is to the Executive Team (E-Team): we will avoid feigned agreement, but once the team has come to an agreement, we will each commit publicly and privately to the decision that has been made—supporting it to all outside the team and working tirelessly to achieve the goals. We should recognize and celebrate successes to maintain high morale both within our area and within the E-team.

4. We commit to accountability within the team, are open about mistakes, and are willing to receive questions from other team members regarding attitudes or actions that may be counterproductive to the good of the team and its commitments.

5. We commit to know what each other is working on so that results of our collective goals will be measured and so that individual goals and those of our various divisions will be secondary in comparison. This may involve sacrifices in individual areas for the overall good of the college.

6. In our interactions, E-Team members will work to create an environment of integrity, care and respect. E-Team members will work to identify and overcome actions inconsistent with our E-Team covenant. We will quickly and genuinely apologize to one another when we say or do something inappropriate or potentially damaging to the team.

7. Regarding our meetings, all members will take an active role in making them compelling and will ensure that the most important issues are put on the table to be resolved; then the meetings will end with specific resolutions and calls to action whenever appropriate.

8. E-Team members will work to create an atmosphere of openness and interest about each other's personal life and family.

What is the purpose of the covenant and our regular interaction with it? It's creating and maintaining the ideals by which we agree to live as an executive team. We do not always live up to the covenant, but our commitment to it establishes the framework for keeping us on track even when we drift from our ideals.

Ultimately, the chemistry of the executive team filters out into the entire organization. But as Drucker so often emphasized, having great team chemistry is secondary to looking outward, where we must achieve results in the organization. In this way the interface of organizational culture with environmental context reminds us that our most important contribution is the one we make beyond the walls of our organization. To develop an enduring, positive, productive organizational culture is obligatory; to ensure that this culture interfaces effectively with our environmental context is not only obligatory but also necessary.

The Quest for Character: Greed Versus Generosity

The character challenge at this level is greed. Greed destroys community. Greed essentially has no limit. Greed is boundless in its grasping for money or fame. Eventually, it leads to a lack of respect for the needs and ambitions of others because our own needs and ambitions overrun all normal boundaries and expectations. It is particularly corrosive on teams, and when present in senior executives, greed can destroy whole organizations. It is made manifest by an excessive need for acclaim, attention or compensation. It also is evident in an inability to share the limelight. Malice and thoughtlessness are twin manifestations of this same inner drive. Its root is a boundless craving that exceeds all capacity for satisfaction.

Generosity, on the other hand, builds community. Generosity allows us to give and receive because we are free from domination by money or fame. Generosity is manifested in our confidence that there will always be enough. It is also a reflection that a senior management team can honor and celebrate the contribution of others and compensate them fairly based on the legitimate value of their contributions. Within generosity is the capacity to self-limit because we do not fear loss of access to resources or opportunities. Generosity also gives us the ability to handle the vicissitudes of life—the ups and downs that come to each one of us—in ways that have a positive and enduring outcome.

Principle 4

THE INTERPLAY OF
CULTURE AND CONTEXT

The Dynamic Relationship of Organizational Culture
and Environmental Context

Increasingly, as the ties of farm and small-town life dissolve,
our knowledge-based society threatens to become rootless.
It needs communities—spheres where the individual can become a master
through their contribution and acceptance of responsibility.

Peter Drucker

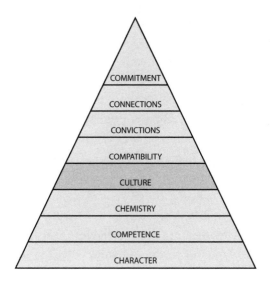

"These flight attendants didn't grow up in the South, so it may be tough." I was on a transcontinental flight from Los Angeles to Atlanta when an employee of Delta Airlines made this comment. Delta had recently acquired another national airline, and he was part of the team responsible for the integration of the two companies. The largest remaining challenge was blending the flight attendants from the acquired company into the culture of the current company. After he summarized his personnel challenges, I had asked him in jest, "Can you make them nice?" His serious answer spoke volumes.

Cultures shape people. What we value, we produce. We are all products of our environment. Not exclusively or exhaustively, but predictably. We display traits that directly reflect the context we were raised in.

I first became interested in the corporate cultures of companies when I was studying cultural anthropology in graduate school. The topics we were studying illustrated how cultures shaped individuals and families, and also indicated the long-term effect these cultures had on societies and organizations.

In the early part of the twentieth century Ludwig Wittgenstein compared the culture of a community to "a big organization that assigns every person a place to work in the spirit of the whole."[1] Clifford Geertz, who followed a generation later, amplified Wittgenstein by noting that a culture forms the "context within which social events, behaviors, institutions, and processes can be understood. It forms the webs of meaning in which we find our significance."[2] These webs of meaning, in turn, help us understand our life. They direct us. They reinforce certain behaviors while eradicating other behaviors. They help us make sense of our life and our world. The same is true of the culture of companies.

In *Built to Last*, Jim Collins and Jerry Porras compare eighteen great companies with eighteen average ones. What distinguishes the great companies from also-rans is the corporate culture of each company. According to Collins and Porras, a healthy corporate culture has four key ingredients: a fervently held core ideology, a process of "friendly" indoctrination, a tightness of fit between the individual and the company, and the cultivation of a spirit of "positive" elitism, in which a person comes to see him- or herself as a special person working at a special place.[3]

Over the past twenty-six years I have worked for five different organizations. Each has had elements of these four characteristics in its culture, but with a unique twist. Each of these five organizations has a core ideology, a process of friendly indoctrination, and an insistence on a tightness of fit between the individual and the organization. In fact, every time there was a bad fit, those individuals self-selected out. What I have found especially interesting, however, is that each of the five organizations did not necessarily exhibit a sense of positive elitism so much as exhibiting a sense that it existed to do something unique that no one else was doing. This sense of "positive purpose" has been deeply motivating.

The Development of Organizational Culture

More recently, scholars in various fields, including organizational psychology, social psychology, neuroscience and communication theory, have turned to analyzing the role and influence of organizational culture.[4] The range of interest is so broad and complex that it cannot be summarized easily. Nevertheless, various threads emerge that help us weave together a tapestry of meaning to guide us.

Symbols, rituals, language-use and stories shape organizational culture.[5] Books such as *In Search of Excellence, Corporate Cultures* and *The Character of Organizations*,[6] help us understand how organizational cultures guide their companies. Ultimately, organizational cultures help us understand how to make our contribution to the companies we strive to serve.[7]

Of course, there are multiple approaches to the study of organizational culture. In general, most approaches belong to one of three broad perspectives: practical, interpretive, or critical and postmodern.[8]

Organizational cultures help us understand who we are,[9] where we can contribute and what we can do.[10] They manifest the observed behaviors, the evolving norms, and the dominant values of the organization.[11] I have come to believe that the CEO and the top management team play a key role in shaping the culture of the company by embedding and transmitting their organizational culture in the following six ways:

- The priorities they set

- The benchmarks they measure

- The response they make both to opportunity and crisis (including organizational crisis due to a stagnant culture)

- Their direct and indirect role modeling of appropriate behavior

- Their philosophy of reward and compensation

- The ways they recruit, select, promote, retire and transition (or allow to be transitioned) members of the organization

Understanding organizational culture is also essential when working crossculturally. The average college graduate today will have anywhere from fourteen to nineteen different jobs during their adult working life, with at least one major assignment outside the United States. With the rise of global commerce and the explosion of interest in outsourcing and off-shoring, the ability to work effectively in the global economy has become imperative. To equip work associates for this reality, we have to train them to be effective crossculturally.[12]

The reality of crosscultural work and communication is captured beautifully in David Livermore's groundbreaking study, which is especially revealing of the challenge we face. The essence of Livermore's work, based on more than twenty years of research spanning twenty-five countries, is the identification of four dominant traits that operate in dynamic tension with one another (see table 4.1). He summarizes his findings in a recently released book, *Leading with Cultural Intelligence.*[13]

Table 4.1. Four Dominant Traits of Cultural Intelligence

Dynamic of Cultural Intelligence (CQ)	Description of Dynamic of CQ
1. CQ Drive	1. The level of motivation we possess to understand, respect and work crossculturally. Our level of motivation will reflect the likelihood of our effectiveness and success.
2. CQ Knowledge	2. The ability to gain an understanding and appreciation for crosscultural differences. How do people learn? How do people live? How do their attitudes, thoughts and behaviors differ from our own?
3. CQ Strategy	3. The ability to use both analytic and synthetic competencies in order to assess the dynamics of your current situation and construct a meaningful response.
4. CQ Action	4. The ability to assess a situation and adapt appropriately.

One of the finest examples of a CEO taking responsibility for embedding and transmitting an organizational culture that transcends cultural boundaries is the life and leadership of Harold A. "Red" Poling, former chair and CEO of Ford Motor Company when it was one of the largest transnational companies in the world.

Harold A. "Red" Poling

I first met Red Poling in 2002. Mike Helmer, a board member at

Spring Arbor University and a longtime friend of Poling's, introduced us. Poling had retired from Ford Motor Company in 1994
after starting at Ford in 1951 and working his entire adult life
within this one company. Because of his rank at retirement (chairman and CEO), Poling was given an office in Dearborn across a
major thoroughfare (M-39) from the international headquarters.
He invited me to meet him once a month for lunch at the Dearborn
Ritz-Carlton, which was connected to his office building by an
underground tunnel. These monthly sessions were some of the
richest moments of my own leadership development and a remarkable tour of organizational culture.

As Poling ascended the ranks at Ford he came under the tute-
lage and guidance of Ed Bundy, a former vice chair and the godfather of corporate careers at Ford. Bundy insisted that Poling articulate his philosophy of management and that he do so in one
page. Figure 4.2 is Poling's one-page manifesto.[14]

Why do I share Poling's philosophy of leadership? In one single-
spaced page we have a gold mine of information on how to be a
great leader. In 2003, Poling agreed to join the board of trustees of
Spring Arbor University. I was president of the university at that
time. As we were preparing to welcome Poling to the board, we
created a fourteen-minute DVD from interviews with a group of
several individuals who had either worked with Poling at Ford or
knew him from his community service and corporate board work
throughout Michigan.[15] The interviewees' stories are priceless and
illustrate how deeply a leader can be loved and respected when
they lead well.[16]

What these testimonials teach us is the way in which Poling
created a culture that was consistent, dependable and predictable.
This, in turn, produced the sort of environment at Ford that contributed to its growth and success. The atmosphere Poling
created, moreover, produced a glorious period in the modern history of Ford Motor Company. This fact reveals that even huge

---

PEOPLE

People are not the Company's most important asset, PEOPLE ARE THE COMPANY. We can meet the objectives, hopes and aspirations of our people if we just TREAT THEM THE WAY WE WOULD LIKE TO BE TREATED.

Trust and *loyalty must be earned*—it cannot be demanded, requested or expected.

What we do speaks louder than what we say. We must keep this in mind in everything we do in regard to our people.

- In remuneration.

- Promotions—individuals must not only have earned a job but must also be perceived to have done so.

- We must listen with an open mind unless our mind is closed, in which case we should so tell our people.

- We should not convey the impression that EI (employee involvement) and PM (participative management—contribution proportionate to responsibility) are substitutions for the right and the responsibility of managers to manage.

- We should not play favorites or be perceived to be so doing.

  - Bad for us
  - Bad for employee
  - Bad for the organization

- We should support our people when they deserve it.

- We should praise in public and critique in private.

- We should strive for contact with our people at all levels—require meeting in small groups.

PRODUCT

Ford's strength in product is "value for money." We need to produce and sell what the consumer wants. We are basically a high-volume producer and have strong appeal to the traditional buyer. We must have the objective of producing the "best quality vehicles in the world and having the world know it." We can lead in styling in certain segments of the market but cannot walk away from our traditional buyer as we are striving for conquest sales. We should be a leader in technology, but be careful not to be so far ahead that we do not have service capability. We should explore niches in the market where we could have an exclusive position or be the first manufactures in that segment.

PROFITS

We are in business to make a reasonable return on investment for our shareholders. It is a fiduciary responsibility. By making a reasonable return, we assure job security and the ability to provide the working conditions and remuneration we want for our employees.

MOST IMPORTANT CONTRIBUTIONS OF TOP MANAGEMENT
Consistency—Dependability—Predictability

Figure 4.1. Red Poling's management philosophy

companies (400,000 plus employees during Poling's time as CEO [1990-1994]) can build great cultures that maximize the gifts and abilities of your people.

Culture and Context

These comments about Poling are instructive. They reflect his commitment to leadership principles that are enduring. They also illustrate Poling's close alignment with principles Peter Drucker often emphasized. For example, Drucker is particularly mindful of the need to create the right culture that can make the worker productive and the work profitable. His development of the key concept of management by objectives (MBO) reflected his core belief that the organizational culture had to be shaped by management directives that move the goals and objectives of work beyond the personalities and politics that so often encumber organizations.[17] Management by objectives makes each manager capable of joint contribution to the company. An organizational culture governed by MBO makes individual contribution possible and collective goal achievement feasible.

A corollary to management by objectives is Douglas McGregor's groundbreaking study on human motivation and work. The architect of the Theory X and Theory Y explanations for motivation and work, McGregor established the basic paradigm for explaining why some managers believe employees enjoy and thrive at work while others do not.[18]

Drucker often touched on McGregor's work in class. He was not a blind advocate of McGregor's findings and even acknowledged some of the study's shortcomings. What Drucker found compelling, however, is the idea that every manager must understand how his or her subordinates work: what motivates them, what discourages them and what drives them to pursue extraordinary results.

We need to study our employees as well. Do we know the right approach in the right situation so that we can maximize the efforts and contribution of our employees?

In addition, Drucker was not only comfortable with shaping the organizational cultures of America's companies, but he also was equally adept at helping Europeans and Asians. He especially enjoyed his involvement with the Japanese. In fact, his love and respect for the Japanese was legendary. Drucker was particularly interested in their practices of "continuous training" and "lifetime employment," which gave individuals and communities the stability they needed to build a great nation as well as a "godfather system" that ensured every employee a mentor who could guide his or her career. These interlocking principles required the employee to strive continuously to improve in serving the evolving needs of his or her company.[19] The godfather system reinforced these two values by leveraging the inherent cultural respect for one's elders with the commitment to mentor and oversee the work of a new employee.

Ultimately, Drucker's ideal work environment is one in which the worker is able to take responsibility for his or her job. Taking responsibility for one's work consists of three primary practices: contributing productive work, receiving real time and continuous feedback, and displaying a commitment to continuous learning.[20]

This type of contribution doesn't happen naturally or even accidentally. It happens intentionally and is the result of a strong organizational culture where good management provides clear direction. It requires a level of stability and security that allows an employee to strive to make his or her best contribution and to have the opportunity to develop.

Because a company is a community, it offers opportunities for leadership responsibility, recognition and learning.[21] This type of organizational culture requires that we grow and change.[22]

To develop a strong culture, leadership jobs should provide our best employees with their brightest opportunities. Drucker was convinced that the trajectory of a company is set by the quality of the top management team. He was especially mindful of how hard it is to hire, develop and retain top management talent and how easy it is to demotivate and drive that same talent away. Designing jobs too small, promoting your top talent to nonleadership roles and refusing to reconfigure "widow-maker" jobs (in Drucker's terminology, jobs that destroy the careers of at least two competent managers in a row) are symptomatic of a deeper divide within a culture.

Ultimately, Drucker's concern was always to develop a culture that produces results. "Morale in an organization does not mean people get along. The test is performance, not conformance."[23] As I've said earlier, I often felt Drucker underestimated the importance of good working relationships. On the other hand, he wanted to be sure that our primary and consistent focus is on results, not just getting along or on activities that are meant to build morale. He believed that a well-running, well-structured organization eliminated organizational dysfunction and gave the greatest and most consistent likelihood of success.

He amplified this point by noting that the structure of an organization fundamentally shapes its culture and that getting the structure right is key.[24] To determine the appropriate structure, seven key elements must be satisfied.

1. Clarity of purpose
2. Economies of scale
3. Direction of strategy
4. Understanding of one's work
5. Clear guidelines for decision making
6. Stability and adaptability
7. Capacity for perpetuation and self-renewal

An established structure provides the culture-shaping guidance we need to understand our key activities.[25] First, we need measurable results. What must we accomplish to preserve the organization and allow it to flourish? Second, what support activities must be executed that in themselves do not produce results but make results possible? What hygiene and housekeeping activities must be fulfilled so as not to derail our core business? Finally, what performance do we need from top management if we as an organization are to be successful?

Form never operates independently of function. These two elements operate in dynamic equilibrium. This is to say, the structure of our organization that creates and reflects our culture is directly influenced by our desired results. Task-focused organizations need a culture that focuses on the best execution of core functions.[26] Results-focused organizations need a culture that allows the greatest freedom and the clearest accountability. Hightouch, high-tech-focused organizations need a systems structure with enough flexibility to make frequent, spontaneous, unplanned meetings possible.[27]

The point with each of these organizational designs is that they constitute the culture of the organization and provide the framework for our work. The objective in finding the appropriate organizational structure is not finding the perfect one but instead finding the one best suited to accomplish our task.[28] As a result, the best organizational design always begins with a clear understanding of the key activities that are needed in order to produce the desired results. An appropriate structure (culture) is the one best suited to maximize the performance of our people. In this way, the culture of the organization helps determine the level of success of the organization.[29]

Culture is shaped in many ways. It receives its initial and formative impulse from the founder and first leadership generation of the company. It evolves over time through the influence, tenure and levels of success of key employees. Organizational culture then continues to be shaped and influenced, especially by the CEO, the top management team, the board of directors and key opinion leaders within the company.

Organizational culture is also shaped and influenced by the environmental context in which it exists. Organizations, like individuals, exist in communities. They have social impacts and are influenced by surrounding social problems.[30] Drucker always kept one eye on the organizational culture and another eye on the environmental context.

In 1989, he released *The New Realities*, a book devoted to identifying and exegeting the dynamics of organizational culture and environmental context on a global scale.[31] This is Peter at his most fascinating. He demonstrates in successive chapters why social and political landscapes change, how twentieth-century civilization had given up on the political movement of salvation by society, the failure of government to deliver on their promises for social advancement, the inability of European socialism and Soviet communism to solve society's persistent social problems, and how new eras emerged without any regard for historical time lines. The book also contains his famously accurate prediction that the Soviet Union was nearing its collapse. He anticipated and identified many positive developments, including the move to "reciprocity" and agreements of mutual benefit as the social currency of the new world order.[32] He identified education as the fundamental value in the new order and the one most able to provide access to any number of jobs now associated with the "knowledge society."[33] This, in turn, has allowed for the emergence of the single-focus, multi-institutional society.[34]

But most impressive is Peter's demonstrated ability to assess and communicate the realities of the world around him. His remarkable insights demonstrate both the importance of paying attention to one's environmental context and the benefits of doing so. If we ever want to truly understand the culture of our organization, we must also seek to understand the environmental context in which it exists.[35]

Gathering Information from the Environmental Context

One of the great mistakes companies often make is to believe that, and behave as if, context doesn't matter. This is when a company operates on the basis of what it prefers and how it believes a society should function, rather than how the society actually operates.

A critical component of understanding organizational culture and environmental context is found in Robert Wuthnow's landmark study *Communities of Discourse*. Here, Wuthnow identifies the eight primary spheres that shape every society and culture (see table 4.2).[36] These spheres form a "community of discourse," a general term he coined to describe the way in which communities originate, change and experience renewal. Anything that people use to communicate —including verbal, written and nonverbal communication, as well as reflection on past experiences—is considered "discourse."

Wuthnow's eight primary spheres demonstrate the key elements that structure a society and illustrate the various elements that must be coordinated for a society to function well.[37] By integrating these different spheres into a meaningful whole, Wuthnow offers insight into why countries and civilizations differ so dramatically throughout history.

Why is Wuthnow's work important? Because the context in which an organization functions will fundamentally shape the organization itself. One example of the impact of this is found in the unique challenges we face in the environment around Westmont College. Our college is located in Santa Barbara, California. Technically, it is in the unincorporated area of Montecito. When I interact with presidents from other institutions, they always have good advice as to how we should proceed with our building plans. But their advice always fits how they would build in their neighborhood, not how we are allowed to build in our neighborhood.

Table 4.2. Wuthnow's Eight Primary Spheres

Eight Primary Spheres	Definitions
1. Social Sphere	Constructed by two primary factors: the environmental conditions and the institutional structures, primarily governmental.
2. Economic Sphere	Includes a review of the production capacities within the society and the way in which the society institutionalizes decisions about these capacities. It also includes the establishment of a central bank, the regulation of the key elements of economic policy and the governance of the money supply.
3. Political Sphere	Concerned with the massive responsibility of integrating and maintaining a diverse population through appropriate institutions that support and reinforce self-governance and bring stability to society.
4. Religious Sphere	Focuses on how religion is institutionalized with a culture.
5. Deviance Sphere	Deals with how the culture defines and responds to deviance. The way deviance is identified, addressed and punished will define the broader social forces at work in society.
6. Cultural Sphere	Integrates the contributions of art, education, entertainment and leisure and how these cultural values influence each society. Societies construct their interpretive frameworks and collective commitments in unique ways that must be understood.
7. Military and Police Sphere	The military and police sphere deals with the role of the police and the military in structure and activity of each society.
8. Legal Sphere	The legal sphere deals with the way in which the judicial and legal institutions of a society are coordinated and interact.

For example, when I was at Spring Arbor University in Michigan, a campus master plan was a straightforward process that often included a beneficial partnership between the county and the university. Conversely, in the context of Santa Barbara generally and Montecito specifically, nongrowth attitudes persistently affect the college. One serious result is a campus master plan process that would typically take six to twelve months has ended up taking seven years. Moreover, every building approved for construction has had to have a letter guaranteeing that the financing is lined up to complete the project. And to add another layer of complexity, the window of opportunity for constructing all the buildings opens and shuts within eighteen to thirty months of obtaining the first building permit. Clearly, building in Montecito is different from building almost anywhere else. The overarching importance of this insight for leaders is that we have to learn our contexts in order to lead our organizations effectively.

Two other notable examples come to mind: funerals in the Midwest and appropriate business attire in the West. When we first moved to Michigan, one of the longest serving faculty members at Spring Arbor passed away. Having never lived in the Midwest, we didn't realize the significance of "the viewing," the custom of displaying the deceased body at the funeral home and visiting with the family a few days before the memorial service. To us, a viewing had always been restricted to the closest members of the person's family, so we skipped the viewing and attended the memorial service, expecting to have a chance to express our condolences to the grieving family. But no opportunity came. As the service ended, the family was whisked away for the private burial at the nearby cemetery. Thankfully, the family was very forgiving and this oversight didn't cost us credibility in the community.

The contrast between cultures regarding business attire is also illuminating. Having lived on the East Coast and then in the

Midwest, the guidelines were always more formal than on the West Coast. This is a good thing in both directions! In the Midwest, respect is communicated in part by how you dress. In the West, respect is communicated much more subtly. What can seem inappropriate to a person from the Midwest is simply a casual culture dressing for comfort.

Integrating Organizational Culture and Environmental Context

How then can we develop an organizational culture that embodies universal ideals? Having worked in several organizations and even outside the United States for a brief time, I have discovered a set of priorities that transcend cultural boundaries.

First and foremost is the recognition that at the heart of every great institution are its people, the primary resource that determines an organization's success or failure. Developing a culture that can grow and sustain people is critical for the long-term success of an organization.

This first priority is built on the equally powerful understanding that every one of us has gifts and abilities, and that it is our responsibility to express these gifts and abilities for the greater good. Our goal at Westmont is to maximize the enormous potential of our people. We want them to understand how they are wired and what they are best equipped to do. We want them to experience the joy of being part of a community that provides the right balance of challenge and support. We want to find meaning in our work by utilizing the principles of emotional intelligence. We also want to benefit from the tremendous intellects of our entire educational community.

As a result, to be effective, leaders need to know themselves and their people. This knowledge requires both the development of self-awareness and the personal discipline of self-reflection. Through this discipline, we develop a capacity to answer the questions that reveal the most about us: *What am I good at? What do I enjoy doing? What am I planning to do in the immediate future? What are my long-term hopes and dreams? Who are the most important people in my life and why?* Effective leaders also take an active interest in those under their care. This develops as a result of spending time with them while seeking to understand and empathize with them. It requires that we not only enjoy our people but also that we learn the emotional cues that different individuals send. This recognition returns us to Drucker's principle of focusing on another person's strengths rather than taking up a critical spirit of judgment on his or her weaknesses. Ultimately, it requires that we be open to mentoring those who need and desire it.

In addition, effective leaders set the emotional tone for the organization. Achieving this desired effect requires self-control and self-regulation. It also requires that we learn how to be good listeners and even better observers. Learn how to anticipate what is happening in the lives of the people under your care. Figure out how to engage the other person's interests. We need to convey the sense that the person we are speaking to is the most important person to us in that moment. In order to set the emotional tone, we must also develop a capacity to manage our internal states, impulses and drives in a way that respects the employees of our organization while channeling our energies in a way that maximizes our effectiveness as a leader.

Closely allied with this priority for tone-setting is the need to be consistent, dependable and predictable. Our employees need to know they can rely on us. They need the assurance that we will do what we say and are true to our word. They need to know that the rewards for their work will be consistent and based on a drive for excellence and success.

In addition, effective leaders know what success looks like and are motivated to achieve it. For the purpose of leading a college, success is about managing resources and giving students the greatest opportunity for transformation. This kind of management requires that we coordinate several components of the organization effectively, including balancing the commitment to a great faculty with a robust student life program that develops the whole person. This balance occurs when our faculty have the resources they need, the quality of students they desire and the financial resources of the college that are sufficient to provide attractive working conditions and fair compensation.

The level of alumni engagement is also a critical benchmark of institutional success. Their level of satisfaction and participation is significant to the long-term influence of the college. Other priorities further removed from the students themselves but still quite important to the life of the college include sound financial management, a strong balance sheet, programs that generate a positive net return and programs of excellence.

Communicating expectations and offering guidance and support also distinguish effective leaders. The Gallup Organization conducted extensive research on the best places to work.[38] This material was analyzed and critiqued in *First, Break All the Rules*. One of the most interesting pieces of this entire study is the demonstration that a willingness and ability to communicate expectations was one of the most significant determinants of employee satisfaction. What Gallup discovered is that employees want and expect to know the following:

- What is expected of me at work?

- In the last seven days, have I received recognition or praise for doing good work?

- Is there someone at work who encourages my development?

- In the last six months, has someone at work talked to me about my progress?

- This last year, have I had opportunities at work to learn and grow?

Effective leaders also know their customers and know their business. Drucker's five key questions help guide our understanding.

- What is our business?

- Who is our customer?

- What does our customer value?

- What are the results we desire?

- What is our plan for achieving these results?

These leading questions not only provide guidance but also help establish our strategy.

Equally important is a consistent focus on customer satisfaction and loyalty. When I was studying marketing, one of the most important statistics that stood out to me is that it is five times more expensive to get a new customer than to retain an old customer. IBM discovered that for every one person who complains, twenty more are dissatisfied. Additionally, while those who are satisfied will tell eight to ten others, those who are dissatisfied will tell eighteen to twenty others. Focusing on customer satisfaction cultivates loyalty. Disney has a remarkable reputation for customer satisfaction that elicits loyalty. So too does Nordstrom.

Think about your favorite memories of customer satisfaction, and think too about your worst memories when you were totally frustrated. What in the first instance makes you want to return to those experiences? In contrast, what in the second instance makes you never want to revisit them?

Effective leaders must also learn to trust and delegate—and we have to be able to trust in order to be able to delegate. One of my favorite stories in all literature is that of Moses' father-in-law Jethro helping Moses delegate his judicial responsibilities by establishing a lower court. The story is found in Exodus 18 of the Old Testament and is one of Dr. Sample's favorites, which he uses in his executive leadership class at USC. You may know the story and recall the dilemma that Moses faced: he was listening to minor court cases every day and getting weary in the process. Jethro intervened, telling Moses to instruct people in the law, to help them become self-reliant, and to train up a whole cadre of people who could adjudicate these lower court proceedings. It is a classic story of delegation, and it illustrates the way that we must focus on getting the right work done in the right way.

Delegation is also the way we fulfill our responsibility to make the strengths of others effective. Ultimately, we have to determine what can be delegated and what we have to handle ourselves. The items that need to be handled personally include confidential matters, disciplinary actions, ceremonial responsibilities, legal matters and final accountability to our board of directors.

These priorities also help us recognize that effective leaders build effective teams and foster teamwork. Leaders are responsible for maximizing the strengths of others for the good of the organization. They must work to remove the obstacles that prevent their employees from doing their best work. Leaders need the opportunity to do what they do best every day. They need to generate assets that ensure the long-term financial viability of the organization. Ultimately, they need to create a values-based organization that will continue the rich cultural tradition after they are gone.

Great teams are a byproduct of effective leaders. They are person-centered, customer-focused and results-oriented. They collaborate with the effective leader in nurturing an institutional culture that gathers momentum based on vision, strategy and carefully conceived directions and plans. Great teams show a capacity for interpersonal understanding. They exhibit high degrees of cooperation. They provide open channels of communication. They have a drive to improve. They are self-aware. They are flexible without being indifferent.

Ultimately, effective leaders create a culture of effectiveness and success. How is this accomplished? It requires that we recognize, develop and demonstrate the appropriate attitudes, behaviors and conduct. The appropriate attitudes include mutual respect, a positive and trusting posture, and an empowering spirit that makes others feel free to contribute. This, in turn, leads to behaviors that reinforce these attitudes as well as to conduct that reflects positive, optimistic points of view.

In the final analysis, the quality of every organizational culture will rise and fall on the quality of the people who inhabit it. In Ken Blanchard's book *Whale Done!* a book that looks at human motivation through the eyes of training killer whales at Sea World, Blanchard notes that the secret to a healthy, vibrant culture is focusing on the power of positive relationships, highlighting people when they are doing the right things and redirecting all energy to positive outcomes.

If you have ever visited Sea World, you know what an awe-inspiring experience it is to see the killer whales perform for the crowd. These massive beasts turn on a dime at even the most subtle command from their trainer. Blanchard's point in highlighting this training is the reminder that we all respond well to positive reinforcement. In fact, we respond best to positive reinforcement, and we should deploy it as our most consistent form of motivation.

In the August 14, 2010, issue of the *Wall Street Journal* a wonderful article documented that the qualities which tend to get people promoted today (integrity, graciousness, honesty, being predictable, etc.) are very different from the Machiavellian characteristics made popular for so many generations. It may seem difficult to create or even impossible to sustain, but the achievement of a great culture is the enduring power of all great companies. Of course, we must feel compatible with this culture for us to work well, and it is this dynamic that is the most significant if we are to maintain our motivation over time.

The Quest for Character: Anger Versus Mildness

The character challenge at this level is anger. Anger is a disorienting emotion: at times it seems appropriate, but it often becomes abusive. Anger arises from a sense of violation—a violation of self, of agreements, of principles. It also arises when we feel a threat to our social status or a desire to control other people's lives. Evagrius defines anger as "the most fierce passion." In fact, it is defined as a boiling and stirring up of wrath against one who has given injury or offense. It tends to lead to a preoccupation with the one we are angry with. It ruins our health—both physical and mental.

Anger can arise when the cultural norms that are meant to regulate an organization are violated on a recurring basis. It results from our own sense of violation. So often in business, individuals get into trouble when they ignore the cultural norms that allow everyone to make their contribution to the whole. We need to pay attention to what makes us feel anger, but we also need to recognize the deeper dynamics at work in order to avoid blowing up. When we take time to excavate the motives behind our anger, we begin to see the deeper dynamics at play in our leadership and organization.

Mildness, on the other hand, is the capacity for self-restraint. The cultivation of mildness helps us recognize the deeper dynamics at play within us and around us, and to maintain our emotional and intellectual equilibrium despite our circumstances. Whether a principle has been violated or we simply feel a great frustration with our situation or ourselves, we can respond with mildness because we have confidence that the principles of integrity, care and respect will prevail.

The greatest source of anger in most organizations is the lack of a predictable, dependable and consistent culture that can guide our interactions and resolve our unmet expectations. Once we recognize such underlying realities, we as leaders have the responsibility to address these recurring problems and move the organization beyond them.

Principle 5

THE STRENGTH OF COMPATIBILITY AND COHERENCE

Discovering the Right Fit

Most Americans do not know what their strengths are. When you ask them, they look at you with a blank stare, or they respond in terms of subject knowledge, which is the wrong answer. . . . The final requirement of effective leadership is that a leader's actions and a leader's professed beliefs must be congruent, or at least compatible.

Peter Drucker

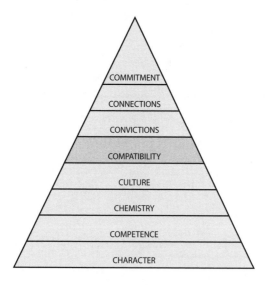

COMMITMENT

CONNECTIONS

CONVICTIONS

COMPATIBILITY

CULTURE

CHEMISTRY

COMPETENCE

CHARACTER

"Eventually, you need to decide where you want to make your contribution. It isn't so much what you do or how you do it, but that you work to make a difference in the lives of people." This insight from Peter Drucker was the essence of our conversation during the fall of 1990. I had written him a brief note trying to figure out what I should do with the rest of my life, and he had invited me to lunch at a local restaurant in order to talk.

I loved the conversation. He cited past conversations he had enjoyed with great thinkers and chided me in a fun way for studying "the Neo-Pagans," the modernist philosophers and theologians who had done so much to undermine our confidence in God. He mentioned his own translation of key nineteenth-century texts (Kierkegaard, etc.) as well as his great admiration for medieval theology (esp. Bonaventure).

At the heart of Drucker's leadership philosophy is the belief that we must understand who we are and how we are wired if we are to understand what we should do. We must work to "know thyself," as the ancient Greeks espouse, and to use this self-knowledge to maximize our strengths. Each individual also needs to consider what contribution he or she can make that no one else could make. Then, upon understanding the contributions we are to make, we need to consider the context in which we should make them.

Answering these questions and others like them should drive us to identify and develop the unique talents and abilities that lie within us. Among Drucker's many perspective-altering principles (including picking the best people, focusing on opportunities rather than problems and being customer-centered rather than product-centered), Drucker's own preoccupation with identifying and utilizing our strengths has been revolutionary.

Prior to Drucker, a disproportionate amount of professional development focused on overcoming our weaknesses. Drucker shifted the focus to maximizing our strengths and minimizing our weaknesses in order to make the greatest contribution possible.

How then do we identify our strengths? Drucker recognized that although we are often inclined to believe we know what we are good at, we are frequently wrong.[1] It is difficult for us to identify and utilize our strengths because we are so often being criticized for our weaknesses. When I was studying with Drucker, he exhorted us, as emerging leaders, to be patient with our current bosses. For the most part, he mused, we were going to be very frustrated because we were working for people who still had a "command and control" approach to their work. He was absolutely right. "Always work for people who will focus on what you can contribute, not on what you did wrong," he would emphasize.

The key to finding our strengths lies in the simple yet difficult exercise of the feedback loop. Begin by writing down what you expect to be the outcome of a decision you are making. Then, at appropriate intervals, review the personal memo to see how close you were to the actual result. By comparing the results with our expectations, we begin to see patterns emerge that demonstrate the best use of our gifts and abilities.

1. What are your strengths?
2. What can you do to increase your performance and expand your productivity?
3. Where does your own arrogance blind you to ways in which you could improve?
4. What bad habits do you need to overcome?
5. What are you doing to focus on your strengths?

Frankly, it is probably overly optimistic to believe that we could analyze and understand ourselves sufficiently to make these adjustments. Still, we need to realize that we must grasp the best expression of our strengths if we are to realize the greatest fulfillment of our contribution. What process is suited for this purpose?

Drucker offers a deliberate process of answering five questions in ever increasing levels of specificity.

First, what are your strengths? Write them down. Always begin with this optimistic belief that we can know ourselves, that we can know we are gifted and that we are all gifted to do something unique that will make a fundamental contribution to the greater good. If we fail to develop and maximize our strengths, our necessary contribution will be lost, and this will be a real loss to our organization and to our society.

Second, once we understand our strengths we need to work to improve them. What can you do to increase your performance and expand your productivity? Do you set goals and pursue development opportunities that you know to be congruent with your greatest talents and abilities?

Third, following the identification and elaboration of your gifts as well as a plan to broaden their development and impact, identify where your own arrogance blinds you to ways you could improve further. One way to break through ego-centrism and arrogance is to utilize an intake instrument or process that incorporates a 360-degree feedback loop, the process where people from all levels of the organization provide feedback.

In my own experience, 360-degree feedback has had limited value. The process has been able to provide an adequate sense of how I am fitting in, but has not been able to identify and elaborate on my greatest strengths or how best to maximize them. What I have found useful is a targeted 360-degree evaluation. If you are stuck using a 360-degree instrument, then make the evaluation beneficial by choosing the individuals who will evaluate you and conduct 80 to 85 percent of the evaluation in the open with the names of the evaluators attached to their feedback.

What I have found in this respect is that the feedback is much more constructive and not given to generalities that sometimes completely miss the point. Allowing a portion of the feedback instrument to be confidential also permits interested parties to register concerns without fear of recrimination or disruption to their own leadership responsibilities. This permits the overwhelming portion of the evaluation to focus on maximizing strengths and the remaining 15 to 20 percent to center on staffing around weaknesses.

Fourth, a corollary to overcoming our arrogance is a commitment to removing bad habits.[2] Bad habits are not the same thing as weaknesses. A weakness is something we cannot help. It is the opposite of a strength or talent: to have a weakness is to admit that we are unable to perform certain functions. A bad habit, on the other hand, is the result of poor manners. It results from lack of discipline, not lack of effort. Bad manners often ruin great opportunities. They undermine our strengths by violating the values and norms of human interaction, and they often contribute to one of the most significant career-limiting mistakes, violating the norms and values of an organization's culture.

Fifth, having identified areas of low capacity, spend as little time as possible working in these areas where your contribution will make the least amount of impact. Such work will simply frustrate you and stymie the needed contribution. Focus on strengths and hire great people in the areas of your organization's most glaring weaknesses.

After identifying our strengths and hiring to remedy weaknesses, we as leaders then need to figure out how we perform. One of the most significant priorities is determining how we like to receive information. This is tied directly to how we learn and how we remember.

Once we have determined how we learn, that is to say, how we receive and process information (by reading, listening, talking, participating, seeing or a combination of all five), we next need to determine how we transmit information. *What is the best way to* communicate great accomplishments? How should we announce disasters? What is the most effective way to communicate positive news, negative news or informative news? The way we process information is often the best way to present information.

The third category, our values, is the ultimate test for what we should do and where we should do it. The risk of moving between organizations is that we really don't know the organization until we are in it. As a result, we can end up in a new situation without the requisite values to sustain us in the job. Of the five different organizations where I have worked, two have ended up having limited opportunities for growth and development. Because lifelong learning and continuous development are values of mine these positions became limiting factors that motivated me to pursue new opportunities with different organizations.

The fourth category, where we belong, dovetails beautifully with the third. In fact, when we have answered the first three priorities—what are your strengths, how do you perform and what are your values?—you have largely answered the questions of the fourth priority, where you belong.

Having changed organizations several times, I have had an opportunity to think through these priorities more than once and determine what would be the best investment of my talents for the next season of life. This process has never been an easy one. In every case, I left situations that were going extremely well with long-

1. Does the new opportunity fit your values as well as your current situation?

2. Is it the right thing to do, for the right reason?

3. Is it timely?

4. Do you have a growing sense you should move to the new position?

5. How do your closest friends think and feel about the opportunity?

6. Do you have a growing passion for the new position?

term horizons in front of me. So how did I decide to move to a new challenge? Here are my six checkpoints.

First, does the new opportunity fit your values as well as your current situation? There has to be value alignment for me to feel engaged in my work. On average, presidential appointments last less than five years; as a result, there is a lot of turnover. This instability leads to frequent queries regarding availability and interest in different opportunities. Once we move beyond the flattery that comes from knowing we are wanted, we realize that most opportunities fail to meet this first threshold test—that is, they fail to align with life values as the kind of organization in which we would want to invest our gifts.

Second, is it the right thing to do, for the right reason? In other words, is the position you are considering a good fit, and is the context you are in at a transition point? Most importantly, does the organization operate with standards of integrity you respect? Was the previous leader handled with integrity, care and respect? Remember: the way the organization treated your predecessor is the way it will eventually treat you. Like individuals, it is only a matter of time before the ingrained tendencies of organizations resurface, and we see deeper realities come to light.

Third, is it timely? Is the work you are doing coming to an end and the work you are being invited to join opening to a new opportunity? This consideration is especially important when considering the long-term impact on your decision to leave you current position. When I was first being recruited by Westmont, I had not finished a major capital campaign at Spring Arbor, so I was unable to pursue Westmont's hiring process to its conclusion. By the time Westmont had pursued other candidates and then reopened the presidential search, I was finished with Spring Arbor's capital campaign but was embroiled in an employee situation that was very complex.

As I reflect back on that time, I realize now why I felt free to leave Spring Arbor while facing the possibility of a protracted legal situation when I had not felt free to leave when the capital campaign was still underway. What I have recognized is that abandoning a capital campaign puts an entire project at risk and can even do harm to the institution for several years to come. Legal issues, on the other hand, can be resolved in a matter of weeks and become nonissues before the leader even leaves town, which happened to me. The public part of the employee issue started in mid-January and was resolved by early March. Conversely, the completion of the capital campaign may have been postponed indefinitely had I not stayed to see it to the end. It is important to discern the difference between circumstances that are situational and temporary and those that are symptomatic and enduring.

Fourth, do you have a growing sense you should move to the new position, or is there an equally strong pull to stay put? I have been approached on several occasions with new opportunities when it was obvious that the situation or the timing discouraged a move. In those times it was very clear I was to stay. Likewise, however, when it was time to leave, it was equally clear that the time had come to go.

Often senior executives leave too soon. The pace of the job and the multiple constituencies that need our attention cause us to lose perspective. This loss causes us to underestimate both the value of the work we are doing and the level of effectiveness we are achieving. In these times my mentors have helped me see that I am making a lasting contribution and have kept me on track even when progress seemed hard to measure.

Fifth, how do your closest personal friends think and feel about the opportunity? Close friends who know our strengths and weaknesses help us determine whether a new opportunity is something we should pursue. All of us need people who look out for us and have our best interests at heart. I have two such individuals in my life. Every time I have made a vocational move, I have discussed it at length with each one of them. Without fail, their sense of when to move and when to stay put has been flawless.

Sixth, do you have a growing passion for the new position? Top leadership positions are exhausting. So often people think they want to be in top leadership positions until they are in them, and then they wish they could return to simpler lives. For some reason the only part of the job people notice is the part that appears to be glamorous. This is probably less than 3 percent of the job. What is often overlooked is the tremendous toll it takes on us personally and on our family corporately. We have to be convinced that we are making the right move because when the challenges come, and they are sure to come, we have to be convinced of our discernment or else the turbulence in the new situation will haunt us.

Of course, there are many other considerations to weigh:

- Where will my family flourish the most?

- Where will I have the greatest opportunity to spend the right amount of time with my family?

- In which situation will I have the opportunity to do what I do best the most often?

- In which situation will my gifts be embraced and celebrated?

- In which situation will I have the greatest opportunity to pursue my vision for the organization?

- In which situation will I experience the greatest congruity between my life values and the values and purposes of the company?

These and many other questions arise as we work our way to understanding where we can make our best contributions. Still, we often need help understanding what these contributions should be and where we should make them. Recent work to answer this question has been undertaken by the Gallup Organization and summarized in StrengthsFinder.

First, Break All the Rules

In 2001, the Gallup Organization released the findings from their landmark study with the Toyota Corporation that resulted in the development of StrengthsFinder, the program and intake instrument that identifies the five dominant themes of employee motivation and works to align talents and abilities with work responsibilities. Under the title *Now, Discover Your Strengths,* Marcus Buckingham and Donald Clifton followed up on their original study with a profile of how we could understand and apply our discovery of strengths to our work as employees.[3]

After we have identified our personal talents, we then need to identify a place to work that will allow us to maximize our contribution through their deliberate deployment. The goal is to move toward more complete alignment of compatibility and coherence. When the Gallup Organization was first developing this instrument, they were also working to determine which values and priorities are present in organizations that emphasize personal talent and contribution. This first study, released under the title *First, Break All the Rules,* identified twelve questions that determine the best places to work. Here are the questions that help make this determination:

1. Do I know what is expected of me at work?
2. Do I have the materials and equipment I need to do my work properly?
3. At work, do I have the opportunity to do what I do best every day?
4. In the last seven days have I received recognition or praise for good work?
5. Does my supervisor or someone at work seem to care about me as a person?
6. Is there someone at work who encourages my development?

7. At work, do my opinions seem to count?

8. Does the mission of my company make me feel like my work is important?

9. Are my coworkers committed to doing quality work?

10. Do I have a best friend at work?

11. In the last six months have I talked with someone about my progress?

12. This last year, have I had opportunities at work to learn and grow?

These questions were selected from a list of hundreds of questions precisely because they identified what made people feel valued and needed in their place of employment.

The purpose of such analysis is to illustrate how critical it is that we identify and develop individual talent. The development of individual talent is not enough, however. If our work and motivation are to be sustainable, talent development must be combined with aligning our life values with the values and purposes of the organizations we serve. I first came to understand this truth from the influence of two key mentors.

Experiencing Compatibility and Coherence Through Community

I first learned the lesson of compatibility and fit from Dr. Alvin Roberts. Not counting my father, Roberts was the first mentor to make a profound and lasting impact on me. We first met during the summer of 1979 when I worked in Medford, Oregon, where Roberts was a medical doctor. By the time I returned for a second summer of work (1983), he had contracted a form of cancer from which he would eventually die on Easter morning, 1986.

Immediately following World War II, Roberts was assigned to postwar Tokyo to treat GIs stationed there. During this time, he resolved that if he ever had a chance to return to a small Quaker community like the one he was raised in, he would jump at the opportunity. He had a wisdom and understanding of life that remains unparalleled. He was quiet and soft-spoken by temperament, but absolutely clear in what he valued and believed.

Our conversations ranged from how to pick a life mate—spiritual compatibility, intellectual compatibility and physical attractiveness—to how we should involve ourselves in organizations that would outlive us. His wisdom and advice centered on the necessity of finding points of compatibility that form the foundation of human relationships and communities. We discussed great literature, how to invest in the stock market, how to pick employees, how to manage our time, how to enjoy lifelong friends (Milo Ross, Jay Allen et al.), how to raise a family, and the joys and limits of physical intimacy. We talked about the necessity of living with fundamental respect for every human being. More than anything, Roberts wanted me to understand that if I was to find enduring happiness in life, I must know myself, what I value and what I believe, and then I must align myself with like-minded people.

Roberts amplified this value by emphasizing how important it was to attend to the uniqueness of every human personality. He used an analogy about a brick wall in which he stressed that trying to move one or two bricks (traits) could cause the entire personality to collapse. We discussed learning to notice what people need most, not what we think they need. And we discussed the necessity of learning to respect people very different than ourselves by considering life from their perspectives.

Roberts had attended St. Louis University Medical School on an Army commission. Following his tour of duty in postwar Tokyo, he returned to the United States and settled in southern Oregon. He had multiple offers to pursue postdoctoral fellowships and even prestigious offers to practice medicine in other parts of the country, but he settled in southern Oregon. He felt the life values he cherished would be reinforced by this region's people and priorities.

From this single decision, Roberts would start a family, build a thriving medical practice, help grow a church and engage in some unusual humanitarian work, including a year-long stint in southern Iran. Being in a less populated and stressful place permitted him to pursue and embrace the full complement of his life values. He often reflected on what might have happened had he gone to a more demanding area where the competition and pace would have destroyed the very opportunities that permitted him to enjoy a full life beyond medicine. My point in highlighting Roberts is he reflects the very essence of how compatibility makes such a difference in the joy we discover in life. We have to know ourselves well enough and understand ourselves deeply enough to enter into the kind of human communities that will sustain us.

Experiencing Compatibility
and Coherence Through Work

Years later, during my first presidency at Spring Arbor, this lesson was driven home again, this time in the personality of Dr. John Beckett. Beckett is the kind of remarkable man that Roberts was. Beckett, now retired from his role as chairman and CEO of the Beckett Corporation in the Cleveland suburb of Elyria, Ohio, is the author of *Loving Monday*. This book tells the story of Beckett's pilgrimage from a bright and promising career as an engineer in the aerospace industry to becoming head of the family business at the age of twenty-six following the tragic death of his father. One of Beckett's first steps was to gain alignment between his personal values and priorities and those of his company.

His wisdom is both timeless and timely. In the late 1990s, he was featured on ABC's *World News Tonight* with Peter Jennings. The focus of the broadcast was Beckett's expression of a "faith at work" theme that captured national attention. Beckett promotes a basic premise: an organization's leader must be very attentive to the hiring process to ensure the company is hiring for compatibility and fit. Beckett views this "gate-keeping" role as critical to providing strong alignment between newly hired employees and the values and priorities of the company. The company's values are explicit: integrity, excellence and a profound respect for the individual. Beckett has observed that in the interview process there are always indicators of how instinctively an applicant aligns with these values. His desire is that from the first interview the company begins to know the basic temperament of each potential employee.[4]

Beyond the individual lies the employee's family. Here, Beckett has crafted some of the most remarkable family-friendly approaches in any industry, including policies that deliberately accommodate the distinct challenges facing new parents. Recognizing the strong and necessary emotional bond that develops between a mother and an infant, Beckett's company allows the new mother to take up to six months' leave in order to help establish this bond. The mother can then work part time or even work at home up to three years to further the bonding process. Of course, the message became clear to all: the company respects not only the individual but their family.

Beyond our individual needs and our family priorities lies our latent talent. Beckett's company offers an educational assistance program that helps individuals pursue the sort of educational preparation that can turn dreams into reality. This three-pronged focus on individual talent, family obligation and continuous growth has engendered a strong commitment by employees toward Beckett. Yet the corporate focus isn't on the impressively low turnover rate. The focus is developing a culture that encourages compatibility and fit, and then hiring the best people who embrace these values. This focus clearly helps perpetuate the company's values while sustaining commitment to the kinds of practices that assure long-term growth and vitality as a company.[5]

Beckett maintains his commitment to allowing the gifts and abilities of his people to determine their best positions at the company. By engaging employees in multiple interviews and by utilizing diagnostic tests, which help match skills and talents to position openings, Beckett fosters a high likelihood of employee compatibility with his company while maximizing their God-given abilities. When we can work for organizations whose core values align so closely with our own, we experience a fulfilling coherence and compatibility with our own life purposes.

In *Good to Great*, Jim Collins emphasizes that we have to get the right people on the bus in the right seats and then build our strategy around them.[6] He claims that if we have the right people on the bus, then the problem of how to motivate and manage people largely disappears. Obviously, if we have the wrong people on the bus, it doesn't really matter if we discover the right direction because we won't have the horsepower to accomplish our vision.

But how do we know if potential employees will be the right fit? In 2009, Nat Stoddard and Claire Wyckoff released *The Right Leader: Selecting Executives Who Fit.*[7] In their work, they discovered the importance of a leader's values, beliefs and personal philosophies in shaping others' character and guiding their motivation. The specific instrument they developed strives to facilitate a match between the executives' values and the culture of the organization.[8]

My Own Experiences of Compatibility and Coherence

Spring Arbor University. In July 2000, Pam and I moved our family to Spring Arbor, Michigan, so I could assume the presidency at Spring Arbor University. We chose Spring Arbor because of the tremendous compatibility we felt with its mission and because of my strong affection and respect for Dr. David McKenna, who was serving as chairman of the board of trustees.

Spring Arbor University is a unique place. My first prominent impression of Spring Arbor is marked by the enthusiasm of my wife to move there. It is part of the folklore of our marriage that the first time we visited campus in January 2000, the trees were bare, the sky was gray, and snow covered the ground. As I remember, it was 8 degrees, with a minus 5 wind chill. In one telling moment of the visit, Pam turned to me and said, "Isn't this great!" And she was serious. But what we also discovered during that first visit was a college community filled with muted hopes and frustrated dreams.

However, from my perspective, whatever frustrations were true of Spring Arbor's present, its future offered tremendous opportunity. Evidence of this opportunity abounded, beginning with the tremendous quality of the people and the collective sense of being committed to something greater than ourselves. The overriding commitment to the Spring Arbor Concept (the mission statement of the university) gave us confidence to move ahead.

Early on we defined the vision for the university to become a top-tier, regional liberal arts university as defined by *U.S. News and World Report*. The goal seemed preposterous to many, but we were convinced that we needed an inspiring goal if we were to break out of our lethargy. In fact, almost every organization and civilization tends to decline the minute it begins to lose its sense of struggle. My overarching vision for Spring Arbor became anchored to key goals that would be articulated in greater depth and clarity over the next seven years.

We faced the need

- to strengthen both the reality and the perception of Spring Arbor University as a top-tier university
- to increase both our total student population and the quality of this student population
- to develop an outstanding executive team that could lead the university during this next phase of development
- to develop and grow the core faculty

- to develop and expand our curriculum
- to build out a robust advancement office
- to diminish our reliance on facilities owned by other organizations by expanding our own campus with new structures, renovating old structures and acquiring surrounding property that would allow this growth and development to occur
- to shift our technology uses from tactical to strategic, and to integrate technology into every facet of the university's work
- to manage our financial resources better
- to become in reality and perception more diverse in ethnicity, gender and geography at every level of the university
- to tell our story better (During my early months at Spring Arbor, I would hear something reminiscent of what one marketing firm said to me directly: "I have good news and bad news; the good news is that everyone who knows you loves you. The bad news is that nobody knows you.")

Finally, we committed ourselves to structured board development following the guiding principles of "best board practices" as defined by the Association of Governing Boards.

The results were very satisfying. Everything that happened began with the development of a great board of trustees. The board of trustees under the leadership of Dr. David McKenna, first, and Les Dietzman, second, displayed the confidence and the willingness to engage in careful but sustained commitments to growth. These decisions did not come easily.

During the seven years of my presidency we took calculated risks based on data-driven decision making. We knew that if we succeeded, we were making decisions that would fundamentally shape and improve the future of the university. In almost every case the calculated risks proved worthy. In addition, the board underwent a transformation as it embraced best board practices that fit the mission and culture of Spring Arbor. These commitments continue to serve the university well, more than four years later.

In 2004-2005, we achieved top-tier status for the first time in Spring Arbor's history. This was the first line of evidence that we had made significant progress in the overall reality and quality of the university. In the next three years the university not only held this position but also fundamentally improved its ranking.

During the 2003-2004 academic year, we won second place in a national competition for Best Places to Work, a study based on the Gallup Organization's nationwide study that surveyed faith-based colleges and universities. Of all the numerous accolades we received, this one was the most meaningful because it documented the headway that was being made in turning the university into an attractive place not only to study but also to work.[9]

Westmont College. Our return to California—specifically, to Westmont College—was filled with intrigue. The hiring process took several months and involved multiple interviews and a sophisticated intake instrument. I was given an exhaustive evaluation that included objective and subjective questions and criteria; according to the consultant, the conclusion of the evaluation showed a strong alignment of my personal life mission with the corporate mission and purpose of Westmont College.

This life and vocational alignment has been so important these past four years. Of all the positions I have ever held, the presidency at Westmont has allowed the expression of the broadest range of my gifts and abilities. Together, my wife Pam and I continue to experience a compatibility and coherence of our life values and our unique gifts that motivates us.

This compatibility and coherence, moreover, has given us the strength to encounter numerous unexpected challenges without being distracted from our core responsibilities. These challenges have included natural disasters (a California wildfire destroyed one million square feet of landscape on campus, burning eight buildings and fifteen faculty homes), the worldwide economic implosion, and predictable organizational stress that comes when senior executives transition. In every case we have been able to weather the storm and provide effective leadership because of the strong support of so many key individuals as well as the strong alignment of our values with Westmont's values. This level of personal and organizational alignment, as well as strong organizational support, is critical for long-term, sustainable success.

The Quest for Character: Pride Versus Humility

The character challenge at this level is pride. Pride is a result of a disproportionate sense of our own contribution, manifested in an inordinate belief in our own importance. Pride is particularly destructive at this level because it causes an individual to believe that his or her contribution as an individual is more important than compatibility with the broader purposes and mission of the organization. Like envy, pride is the inability to value and recognize the contributions of others because it threatens the view we want to hold of ourselves.

Humility, on the other hand, is the result of seeing ourselves properly. It involves recognizing that our gifts and abilities fit into a greater whole. It understands that others have gifts and abilities as well. Humility allows us to see our roles in the greater purposes of an organization without feeling threatened by the contributions of others.

Iris Murdoch once defined the moral life as coming to perceive reality accurately. She went on to define the challenge of the moral life as the challenge to overcome the gravity of our dull, fat, relentless ego. Humility is the antidote for an unbridled ego.

Principle 6

LEADING WITH CONVICTIONS

Making Life's Greatest Impact

Executives in an organization must believe that its mission and task are society's most important mission and task as well as the foundation for everything else. If they do not believe this, the organization will soon lose faith in itself, self-confidence, pride, and the ability to perform.

Peter Drucker

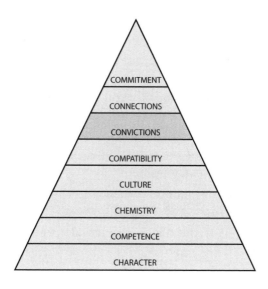

COMMITMENT

CONNECTIONS

CONVICTIONS

COMPATIBILITY

CULTURE

CHEMISTRY

COMPETENCE

CHARACTER

In the early 1980s, Peter Drucker began to turn his attention to the third sector: the nongovernmental, not-for-profit sphere of the economy, which had developed a growing influence in our nation and on our lives. Two key figures played a role in this emerging interest: Francis Hesselbein, then CEO of the Girl Scouts, and Bill Pollard, chairman and CEO of ServiceMaster. Drucker's interest in nonprofits was due in no small measure to the tremendous influence of these individuals and their organizations. He saw in these organizations the effectiveness, efficiencies of scale and motivations of purpose that had gone missing from many of the for-profit and governmental organizations he had worked with.

By the time I was studying with Drucker in 1990, he had already published his book on leading and managing the nonprofit organization. At its heart was a reiteration of his sentiment that for individuals to be motivated and working efficiently, strongly held *convictions* must motivate what organizations are doing.

He also began to elevate the sense of responsibility that organizations must carry for the betterment and social welfare of all society. While studying with Drucker, I first understood that society looks to businesses and organizations to solve all of its problems; society has not lost sight of the role of the individual, but none of us ever makes a contribution on our own. Individual contribution is always tied to the collective contribution made through organizations and businesses. Believing social innovation was even more important than scientific innovation, Drucker laid out six leading convictions that should guide us.

First, every organization has to build the management of change into its very structure.[1] Two competing forces catapult us forward. On the one hand, we need to pursue abandonment of everything that does not fit our core purposes or serve our long-term interests. On the other hand, we need to engage in continuous innovation around our core competencies. These countervailing forces simultaneously create the disequilibrium leading to the next phase of innovation and change while balancing competing forces to propel an organization forward.

I have been in organizations that understand the necessity of innovation and change. The reason I believe Drucker is right is that his underlying assumptions are right: we do not exist in a steady state but rather in a world of perpetual change. This recognition should give us a bias for innovation and change. The organizations that embrace innovation and change will have the energy and the culture to adjust to a changing world; however, those that lack these qualities will suffer and decline.

Recently, I received a copy of "Crafting a Culture of Character" from Bill Pollard. Pollard contributed this article to a *Leader to Leader* issue dedicated to honoring Drucker's one-hundredth birthday (November 19, 2009). Pollard's article identifies and amplifies the way in which Drucker helped him think through his work for ServiceMaster. In one telling example, Pollard recounts the story of going to Japan on a business trip with Drucker only to have his Japanese counterparts fail to show up at an important meeting. In many respects Pollard understood exactly what it meant for his Asian counterparts to stand him up. Pollard's initial reaction, as he recounts it, was to plan to skip a meeting with these Japanese associates the next day and just head home, but Drucker confronted Pollard and emphasized the need for him to take a humble approach in order to restore the relationships for the good of the company. Needless to say, the gesture had an incredibly positive effect and demonstrated both Drucker's courage and Pollard's wisdom in allowing him to make a response that led to a great recovery. The story is one of the most remarkable illustrations of how we can express our convictions while still maintaining our connections for the greater good of the company.[2]

Second, every organization must accept responsibility for its total impact, not just its economic impact. It is absolutely wrong to assess an organization's responsibility as strictly an economic one. Clearly, economic performance is its first responsibility, but it is wrong to assume or assert that profit is its only responsibility. Thus, an organization assumes full responsibility only when it considers its total impact on its employees, on its external environment, on its customers and on whatever else it touches.

Since we have become a global community, we should be acutely aware that what happens in one place on the planet eventually has an effect on every other part of the planet. During the summer of 2010, British Petroleum's ruptured oil platform and drilling station off the Louisiana coast offered a stark reminder that industry has its effects. With eleven workers dead and millions of gallons of oil seeping into the marshes and low-lying coastal areas of Louisiana, Mississippi and Florida, BP's total impact will be felt for years to come.

Third, because modern society is composed of specialists, an organization's mission must be crystal clear. The organization must be single-minded, lest its members become confused. Only a focused and common mission will hold the organization together. Without such a mission, the organization will soon lose credibility as well as its ability to attract the very people it needs to perform.

When I was interviewing at Westmont, I was asked what I could do to assure the board of trustees that we wouldn't wander from our mission. In reality, no single individual or group can fail to uphold the mission statement without this failure having a direct bearing on the organization itself. This responsibility applies to every individual at every level of the organization, including the board itself. The mission of an organization is preserved and extended when we all feel the weight of responsibility to uphold it.

Fourth, organizations must come to terms with the advent of the knowledge worker. With the rise of a service economy tied to a technological infrastructure, workers are increasingly portable. Because organizations are always in competition for people, loyalty can no longer be secured simply by location and a paycheck. As a result, the most successful organizations demonstrate to their knowledge workers that they will offer them exceptional opportunities to grow, to develop and to put their knowledge to work.

In many respects Drucker was a living embodiment of this conviction. Raised in Vienna, he fled to London as Hitler came to power. He once joked in class that his graduate studies concluded when he and his academic adviser agreed they didn't want to see each other any more. From London, he migrated to New York City and eventually to Southern California. In every case, his ability to adapt was a direct result of the portability of his one enormous asset: his knowledge.

More recently, the dramatic changes in higher education, print publication and textbook manufacturing serve as striking reminders of how portable and transient knowledge has become. Online education is now the fastest growing aspect of higher education—allowing people to take classes anytime, anywhere, taught by anybody. *Forbes* magazine, the flagship publication of Forbes, Inc., has its knowledge staff—its senior leadership team—dispersed nationally and internationally. The owner lives outside of Manhattan, the publisher lives on the West Coast, and many of the senior editors and writers live around the world. As I write this book, a Westmont colleague is publishing an online e-book on entrepreneurship and innovation. No print copies will even be produced.

Fifth, having an organization of knowledge workers flattens the organization and requires it be organized as a series of teams. This does not remove the need or place for management. Just as every team has a coach, every organization must be managed. People must be held accountable for the organization's total performance, its adherence to its mission and its ultimate results. Nevertheless, the image of the blustery boss storming around the corporate office demanding results is becoming an outdated phenomenon.

Finally, to perform its mission and fulfill its purpose, the organization has to be organized and managed in a way that shows care and respect for the knowledge worker. This dynamic is crucial. Knowledge workers have become "free agents," able to move between and among organizations based on their unique set of knowledge and skills. In today's economy, "production" is moving from a factory confined by time and place to a knowledge worker available around the clock from anywhere in the world. This change in production has revolutionized business practices: it has reduced multiple levels of the organizational chart while also making organizational leadership and management more challenging.

Because this change in production is relatively new yet so important for long-term success, how can each leader create a climate and culture that maximizes the contribution of the knowledge worker? Early in my career as a college president, I attended a summer institute at Harvard Graduate School of Education. At the institute, I first encountered Dr. Robert Kegan and the ideas captured in his groundbreaking work *How the Way We Talk Can Change the Way We Work*.[3] His seven core principles operate as guiding convictions that can lead a knowledge-based organization.

Changing the Way We Work

Kegan's work unlocks the essence of organizations and pushes us to learn to interact in ways that will be more conducive to our emotional and professional well-being. His work, based on the integration of psychological theories and longitudinal studies, emphasizes the need to change the way we work by reengineering the way we interact. Kegan's work strikes me as remarkably insightful, accurate and helpful. He divides his principles, or governing convictions, into four internal languages (1-4) and three social languages (5-7). Table 6.1 displays Kegan's work.

Table 6.1. Kegan's Governing Principles

Type of Language	Description of Language
1. From the language of complaint to the language of commitment	1. The most dominant form of interaction at work is complaining, but we recognize the more deeply held commitments beneath the complaints.
2. From the language of blame to the language of personal responsibility	2. We stop blaming our problems on external forces and begin to accept personal responsibility for our circumstances.
3. From the language of New Year's resolutions to the language of competing commitments	3. We start off with the energy and interest to change something, but after a few weeks or even a month, competing commitments rise up and undermine our ability to persevere with our new commitments.
4. From the language of big assumptions that hold us to the language of assumptions we hold	4. We often allow ourselves to be captivated by working assumptions that are ill-conceived or mistaken.
5. From the language of prizes and praising to the language of ongoing regard	5. We move from making general and grandiose statements about a person to making comments that are direct, specific and express our appreciation for concrete contributions.
6. From the language of rules and policies to the language of public agreement	6. We move away from long and extensive policy manuals to developing public agreements to which everyone agrees and everyone is held accountable.
7. From the language of constructive criticism to the language of deconstructive criticism	7. All criticism is in some sense negative and demotivating. By contrast, to allow the evaluation process to have incomplete elements, we acknowledge our limited and incomplete view and allow additional information to be shared before we reach our conclusion.

The structure of Kegan's thought is arranged to teach us how to move from one way of interacting and behaving to another. Thus, we first need to move from *the language of complaint* to *the lan-*

guage of commitment. When I first heard Kegan present his theory, I was immediately captivated by this principle. The first principle was the result of a major longitudinal study in which his research team had determined that the most dominant form of interaction at work, even by those who register as "most satisfied," is complaining. In fact, 67 percent of all interaction in the workplace is complaining.

On the surface this seems a depressing conclusion, but Kegan claims that beneath the language of complaining reside more deeply held convictions. At the summer institute he led us through an exercise to help us identify our most dominant complaints and what they reveal about our more deeply held convictions. This intellectual and intrapersonal work helps unveil the motive bases that govern us, often without our awareness. It also sets the stage for the activities of the other six languages. Without treating the full extent of his theory here, we can acknowledge that this first step unveils how presenting problems arise from more deeply held beliefs.

The second principle of internal language is to move from *the language of blame* to *the language of personal responsibility.* This transition is where we stop blaming our problems on external forces and begin to accept personal responsibility. Kegan stresses that though we often believe our problems are beyond our control, we may carry much greater personal responsibility than we first realize.

In fact, this second conviction reflects the inherent human tendency to blame others and external circumstances rather than taking responsibility for the choices we have made. Achieving this second language requires us to answer this question: *What am I doing or not doing that prevents my commitments from being fully realized?* As Kegan led us through this section of our exercise at the institute, I began to realize all the ways that we undermine the very outcome we desire simply because we focus on the presenting problem, not the real problem. Recognizing the extent to which we often sidestep personal responsibility was very sobering. This exercise caused me to focus anew on the power of an organizational culture and my responsibilities within it; I became especially interested in building organizational cultures that would balance a focus on personal responsibility with the need to achieve results.

Following a discussion of the changes advocated by the language of personal responsibility, Kegan explained a reality I have experienced all my life: moving from *the language of New Year's resolutions* to *the language of competing commitments*. This third principle of internal language captivated me immediately. Kegan explained what often happens to people who make New Year's resolutions: they start off with the energy and commitment for significant changes, but about a month into the resolutions, they begin to waffle. This pattern emerges not because people are lazy or unprincipled but rather because competing commitments rise up to sabotage their initiative.

I had never heard this scenario analyzed so clearly and succinctly. Within an organization I often witness an initially high level of energy and engagement for a new priority, yet that intensity diminishes over time. Kegan offers an astute explanation. It is not that a leader loses his or her commitment to a certain priority or a particular course of action; rather, an equally powerful, competing priority stymies that leader.

Once I embraced the concept of competing commitments, I began to experience Kegan's call to move beyond a dynamic equilibrium that creates immunity to change. My focus became striving for a higher level of accountability by recognizing the reality of competing commitments and the recurring tension that comes from embracing such a posture. This third level of organizational understanding continues to guide me and plays a significant role in my own understanding of the dynamics of an organization.

Kegan's fourth principle of internal language is to move from *the language of big assumptions that hold us* to *the language of assumptions we hold.* Initially, this phrasing confused me, and I even thought he had gotten the concept backward. However, over time and through his explanatory help, I have come to realize the power of this fourth principle.

Kegan helps us understand that many of the assumptions that control us are ill-placed and undefined. We often aren't even aware of their influence, yet they play an incredibly powerful role in controlling our thoughts and behaviors. Kegan's process asks us to excavate the assumptions we hold so that we can understand how to maintain our convictions while pursuing innovation and change.

This process is crucial. Too many organizations stall out because they stop looking for ways to preserve their mission while pursuing new opportunities. Too often the past both prevents us from dreaming about the future and paralyzes us so that we are unable to move ahead. For example, consider how your current assumptions are preventing you from innovating in ways that would fundamentally help your organization; then consider how you can both preserve your core mission and extend its reach and influence by embracing innovation and change. Such reflection and change is highly challenging work: you must understand and maintain the essence of your organization while seeing it in a new way.

Many of us are familiar with the two-faced figure from Gestalt psychology: an image that simultaneously shows an old woman looking down and a young woman looking over her own shoulder.[4] The old woman has a scarf covering her head while the young woman has a feather in her hat. It is impossible to see both figures simultaneously, but once we see both figures, our mind and eyes move almost instantly between the two images. In Gestalt psychology, this phenomenon is called "figure and ground." We can never see both figures simultaneously, but our minds and eyes oscillate back and forth almost instantaneously. Kegan's fourth principle works similarly regarding our perceptions of an organization. Moving from the language of big assumptions that hold us to the language of assumptions we hold helps us see the essence of the company while seeing new opportunities. We must develop the capacity to look in both directions without becoming distracted or disoriented.

After detailing the four internal languages, Kegan transitions to discussing the organizational application of these principles along with identifying and elaborating on three social languages. The first social language is to move from *the language of prizes and praising* to *the language of ongoing regard*. The problem here is our tendency to resort to communication and reward systems that are indirect, nonspecific and general.

In discussing the first social language, Kegan identifies a behavior that plagues most organizations: referring to a person as *awesome* or *great* or *fantastic* without stopping to identify the specific traits worthy of such appreciation. Conversely, Kegan emphasizes that we must develop direct and specific language by focusing on individual behaviors and specific contributions. By disciplining ourselves to notice an individual's specific contribution, we help to create a culture of ongoing regard. In other words, rather than saying "Richard is awesome," focus on saying "the way Richard made his commencement address was timely, articulate and persuasive." This language of regard helps us achieve two things: First, Richard feels appreciated for his contribution. Second, he knows why he is being appreciated and is able to replicate the behavior in the future.

Kegan's second social language principle is to move from *the language of rules and policies* to *the language of public agreement*. The emphasis is to create a culture that builds and reinforces organizational integrity. Organizations often become inherently unfair, inattentive and ineffective. Pushing people into public agreements creates a culture of accountability that calls us to more mature behavior.

As Kegan trained us regarding this language, he emphasized how companies and organizations could narrow the size and scope of their policy manuals by creating public agreements with the expectation for every employee to be self-governing. Kegan's expectation that people can live by statements they agree to still intrigues me. His most memorable illustration relates to diminishing if not entirely eradicating backbiting and gossip in the workplace. On the surface this change sounds impossible. However, as Kegan illustrated, your workplace could stop these behaviors immediately if everyone agreed to talk about someone only if he or she was also in the room. Accomplishing this result requires a public agreement that everyone upholds when an individual or a group tries to revert to the natural tendency to gossip.

The final social language is to move from *the language of constructive criticism* to *the language of deconstructive criticism.* This fascinating concept takes a fresh look at the role and value of evaluations. It also requires humility on the part of the observer. Kegan's point is that all criticism, including constructive criticism, is inherently demotivating because the conversation is one way. Often, the target of the criticism is never allowed to put his or her behavior into context.

What I have found especially helpful about this last language principle is its recognition that our perspective is incomplete. Similarly, it leads to an evaluation process that acknowledges we do not have all the information. Engaging in deconstructive criticism—making observations that allow input from the person or situation being critiqued—allows the person being evaluated to share his or her perspective on events, thus offering a more complete picture.

Since learning the principles that make up these languages and studying Kegan's system further, I have tried to implement his ideas at work. The results have been positive but incomplete. No single system is ever sufficient on its own: every organization must contend with the human element, which is unpredictable. What has been helpful, however, is the commitment to creating a common language to guide interactions. Such commitment helps create an organizational culture that is comfortable engaging in deeper thinking about our interaction and its effects.

Ultimately, these seven languages demonstrate how our behaviors have direct social effect on our organizations. In each case these personal and social languages identify and express convictions that produce the most sustainable organization possible. Although I initially learned to recognize the impacts of convictions on organizations from Peter Drucker, and later had this perspective amplified by Robert Kegan, I ultimately saw conviction's full-bodied expression in the life and leadership of Dr. David L. McKenna.

Convictions at Work

Dr. David L. McKenna was president of three institutions; his presidencies spanned a total of thirty-three years. In 2000, while serving as chairman of the board of trustees at Spring Arbor University, he hired me as the twenty-seventh president, a position I would hold from 2000 to 2007. During McKenna's thirty-three years as a chief executive, he formed a series of guiding convictions that now shape his writing and consulting.

At the heart of McKenna's concept of *conviction* is the work of Rabbi Edwin Friedman, who bases his leadership theory on "family systems therapy." In this context the ideal leader is the "self-differentiated leader," one who can maintain an objective sense of what needs to happen while maintaining ongoing relationships with members of the group. In 2005, McKenna published his evolving thoughts on leadership in his book *Never Blink in a Hail-*

storm.[5] In his chapter on how to deal with "toxic people," he uses Friedman's work on holding convictions and connections together extensively.[6]

Although usually treated separately, these two principles operate in dynamic tension with each other. In order to serve as a self-differentiated leader, an individual must balance a strong self-understanding and self-esteem with the necessity of confronting all issues both objectively and subjectively. On the one hand, if a leader becomes too objective, he or she will become isolated from the needs of the people. On the other hand, becoming too subjective means that a leader will become so immersed in the interpersonal relationships that the issues will remain unresolved. Thus, a self-differentiated leader is one who has a head (intellectual capacity) from which he speaks with conviction while having a heart (empathetic capacity) with which he stays connected to people.[7]

Here are the qualities that characterize the self-differentiated leader.

A self-differentiated leader *never loses connectional relationships when making convictional decisions.* This first principle is a challenge that most leaders may have trouble fulfilling. The secret for those who are most successful, however, seems to lie in being able to self-regulate. Mature leaders refuse to be drawn into the drama of office politics. They resist this urge and thus hold their in-

The Self-Differentiated Leader

- Never loses connectional relationships when making convictional decisions
- Never casts blame when stating the case
- Never puts on a gas mask in a toxic environment
- Never creates a triangle (involving a third party) in order to diffuse responsibility
- Never delays direct confrontation when needed
- Never hesitates in dealing with saboteurs

dividual and corporate responsibilities in dynamic tension.

A beautiful example of this practice is Bob Kates, a current board member at Westmont and a former Stanford Medical School professor who left to start his own biotech firm. Kates has the uncanny ability to have a hard conversation without losing a relationship. Even when expressing strong opinions about what needs to be done, he does so with unusual calm and professionalism. Because Kates exhibits a high degree of self-differentiation, he is able to set direction, correct missteps and keep a company on track while still preserving the relationship.

A second principle is that a self-differentiated leader *never casts blame when stating the case.* This behavior is quite critical and relates to our earlier consideration of Robert Kegan's work. Taking personal responsibility releases the organization to hold all workers accountable. When an organization shifts from blame to responsibility, this shift allows all members of the organization to focus on their contribution.

During my studies with Drucker, we read a case study on how President Kennedy handled the Bay of Pigs fiasco. What Drucker wanted us to learn is that even though many of the missteps had nothing to do with the president's own behavior, Kennedy took full responsibility for the operation and its miserable failure. In doing so publicly, he refused to cast blame anywhere else in the chain of command. Off-line, it was a different story. But Kennedy's example shows the right way to handle any major mishap: take full responsibility in public, correct all mishaps in private.

In addition, a self-differentiated leader *never puts on a gas mask in a toxic environment.* This quality is the key for a self-differentiated leader: are we going to continue to put up with dysfunction, or are we willing to address it and remove it? A gas mask is symbolic of people willing to hold their noses and hope a problem will go away. Oddly enough, the more a problem person senses we won't deal with him or her, the more emboldened the person becomes. Every organization in which I have served has had its toxic personalities. They often have self-justifying tendencies and an exaggerated sense of their importance. They are never worth the ruin they bring the company.

In an earlier assignment I experienced this damage firsthand because of my own delay in acting. I had an employee who was toxic to the organization, and I kept postponing the inevitable. Finally, one of the senior members of my team took me to lunch and asked me why I hadn't dealt with the problem. His frankness as well as his blunt documentation of the toll this delay was taking on the team helped me realize the necessity of removing this toxic person from our organization. When I eventually acted, the initial reaction was predictably unpleasant; however, after only a few days without this individual, it was amazing how much better everything worked. As leaders, we have the responsibility to remove individuals who are compromising the work of others and ruining the atmosphere of the company.

A self-differentiated leader *never creates a triangle (involving a third party) in order to diffuse responsibility.* A blame triangle develops when a person wants to pin his or her underperformance or misfortune on someone else. Years ago I worked with an individual who would create blame triangles repeatedly. He would start by asking a question that shifted the focus from himself to another member of the team; the question would always be a loaded one that made it appear that this issue was going to be the rise or fall of the entire organization. Once we realized what was going on, we were able to keep the pattern from recurring, but it proved destructive for several months before we confronted it directly.

In the first full-time job I ever held, I had the privilege of working for a very progressive leader named Jack Willcuts. Willcuts was nearing the end of his career, but his wisdom and sense of timing were remarkable. He insisted on maintaining the highest levels of professionalism in our attitudes and conduct. One of his consistent practices was to shut down any backstabbing before it gathered steam. If someone cast blame on someone else for a mishap, Willcuts's standard approach was to ask the person making the statement to come with him to discuss this with the person who had just been accused. You wouldn't believe how quickly people quit blaming others once they realized they were going to have to own their words in front of the other individual. By practicing the principle that all conversations would be handled directly and with the person named, Willcuts kept the organization from drifting into self-destructive behavior.

This lesson was reinforced when I worked for Dr. McKenna. I quickly learned that he was intolerant of blame triangles. It was a great life lesson, since every organization I have served has had its blame triangles. Individuals and organizations that resort to blame triangles operate in ways that allow individuals to avoid responsibility and organizations to suffer mission drift.

A self-differentiated leader *never delays direct confrontation when needed.* I find this principle to be the most difficult. I would be more inclined to reframe this conviction as *a leader never delays confronting at the appropriate time.* Kegan's emphasis on deconstructive criticism offers an important corrective: before confronting someone, we need to get all the facts. Even then, we need to approach the conversation with a sense of humility, recognizing that we may not have all the information and that there are always two sides to a story. By balancing the conviction that we must confront with the equally strong conviction that we do so deconstructively (taking an indirect, conversational approach), we can maintain the integrity of our leadership while assuring ourselves that we have the most reliable view of our circumstances.

A self-differentiated leader *never hesitates in dealing with saboteurs.* A saboteur is hard to spot initially, but his or her effect is long-term and pernicious. A saboteur simply is someone who engages in sabotage. This final leadership quality is the most difficult for me to resolve quickly or easily. In fact, I'm not sure a confrontation ever ensures the desired result.

Steve Sample, president of USC, has an approach that I find the most attractive. He likes to sit down with a person he has a problem with and express himself to the person in terms of how he sees the situation. He then invites the individual to share his or her view of things. If the person is undermining him or his "chief lieutenants," Sample has little regard and even less patience with keeping that individual on his team. If, however, that person has a moment of insight and understands what new behavior is required, Sample is willing to offer the individual a second chance. This approach seems the most restorative and effective. It allows an individual to submit to correction while keeping his or her job intact. It also allows a president the latitude needed to address issues without every confrontation ending in a dramatic, disruptive termination of a work associate.

Finishing Well

McKenna also taught me the timeless principles of finishing well. Watching senior executives transition provides an interesting study in who has prepared for these changes and who remains unprepared. McKenna always emphasized that we have to prepare for our exit from the day we arrive, and we do it by focusing on the following priorities.

First, leaders must fulfill their responsibility to build upon the history of an organization and contribute significantly to its ongoing story. Holding this priority helps leaders prepare to transition by knowing that they have made contributions that matter. It also reminds us that every contribution we make is built on the backs of those who have gone before us. As Drucker so aptly notes, the defining mark of the twentieth century is the rise of the organization. Organizations define us, and in the process, they give us the opportunity to make a contribution that will outlive us.

Next, to understand the total impact of our organization, we need to contribute to the formation of the culture of the organization: what it is, why it is and where it is going. This emphasis on organizational culture is critical to making a long-term contribution. Organizations develop shared understandings. As noted earlier, these understandings constitute a culture. The culture of the organization guides many of the interactions that happen day-to-day. These interactions evolve over time. They can be changed, but not instantly or dramatically: rather, we should pursue health through gentle, sustained effort. When dysfunction emerges, it is imperative that it be confronted, yet confronting dysfunctional patterns is also dangerous since dysfunctional patterns influence who survives in an organization. To change these patterns and move them to health will threaten the influence of the very people who rely on this dysfunction for their sense of contribution and control.

Once we understand the culture of an organization, we can begin to understand the core beliefs, rites and rituals that help regulate institutional behavior. It is essential that we gain a working knowledge of these unique behaviors as our negotiation of these critical ingredients will influence the whole organization.

After grasping the internal dynamics, we must assess what contribution the organization can make to its respective industry. Effective leaders seek to understand both the general concept of organizational life cycle and the specific applications of this concept to their own organization.

Finally, effective leaders plan their exits in such a way that their departures cast no shadow over their successors. To use Friedman's term, "self-differentiated leaders" celebrate the person, position and promise of those who follow them.

These were lessons I learned from McKenna, and they continue to guide me. Of course, the joy of the job is building relationships day in and day out, year in and year out in the same organization.

The enduring challenge is the responsibility to remain emotionally connected while leading and managing a company to necessary results.

The Quest for Character: Lust Versus Fidelity

The character challenge at this level is lust. Lust is the result of believing that others exist strictly to satisfy our own desires: unbridled sexual desire is but one manifestation of this deadly thought. Lust is basically our entire being run amok. We lose our capacity to maintain any convictions because we are consumed by our drive to satisfy desires that have no end.

Lust is placed at this level because it deals with the incapacity to hold to our convictions. Despite the clear evidence that the quest to satisfy unbridled desires can ruin a career, this deadly thought has led to the demise of more individuals than any other and also has led to more workplace changes than any other. Beyond the impact on workplace policies, lust has the greater effect of undermining the respect and confidence we need from our work associates in order to lead well. Ultimately, lust has to be restrained; ignoring it will cause us to violate appropriate boundaries that are necessary to do our work well and lead effectively.

Fidelity, on the other hand, is the capacity to honor and respect other individuals and the commitments we make to them as much as we desire to be honored and respected ourselves. When we express the qualities of integrity, care and respect, we create cultures that foster fidelity in others. This level of commitment inspires other people to place confidence and trust in us, and to learn to depend on us as we lead and influence the destinies of our organizations.

Principle 7

MAINTAINING OUR CONNECTIONS

Facing Our Greatest Leadership Challenge

*The answer to the question "What is our business?" is neither
simple nor obvious. To raise the question always reveals cleavages and
differences within the top-management group itself. For this reason, it must
be asked, for it enables the top management group to work together precisely
because each member is cognizant of fundamental differences within the
group, and, therefore, far more likely to understand what motivates
his colleagues and what explains their behavior.*

Peter Drucker

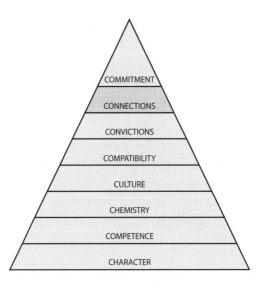

"I understand, but there's nothing about this that feels very loving." I received this response after communicating to a key associate that I didn't think he was a good fit for his position, and I thought we would need to make a change. As we finished our conversation, I had asked him, "Despite your disappointment, are you able to understand why I made this decision, and do you feel like you've been treated with love, integrity, care and respect?" The response he made has lingered in my mind ever since. There is simply no way to transition someone into another position or out of the organization altogether and have that individual feel good about the move. Moreover, the other members of the team take note of our behavior and often have one of two responses: *When will it happen to me?* or *It's about time.*

The people decisions we make have the greatest influence on the trajectory and potential for success of our organization, but how can we stay emotionally connected to our associates while holding the convictions that will drive the company to long-term, sustainable success? This is the essence of effective leadership.

Drucker on Connections

Listening to Peter Drucker discuss the importance of people to an organization is one of the most memorable experiences of my entire career. In so many respects, his human-centered approach to leadership revolutionized the field. How, then, might we bring his thoughts to life today?

The starting point is realizing that a human-centered approach to leadership begins with the right human relations.[1] There are four basic requirements. First, we have to identify and communicate the contribution we want each employee to make. Knowledge workers must know and understand what is expected of them.

Second, we have to motivate and organize each individual's contribution so that he or she can contribute to the whole. Think, for example, of a hospital administrator or an orchestra conductor. In the case of hospital administrators, they are responsible ultimately for patient care and for the restoration of health. All functions within the hospital are focused on that end, and their work is meant to ensure the coordination of all the disparate, individual parts of knowledge into a meaningful whole that can contribute to the recovery of the health of the patient. Similarly, orchestra conductors are not responsible for playing every instrument. They are responsible for ensuring that every instrument is played well. Both analogies illustrate the essence of effective leadership—making joint performance possible by ensuring the superb contribution of each individual according to his or her gifts.

Third, we have to have a plan for self-improvement. In a eulogy for Drucker, Steve Forbes, the CEO of Forbes, Inc., claimed that what made Drucker unique is that he never grew stale intellectually. What a tribute! Drucker was nearly ninety-six when he passed away, yet he never stopped learning and growing.

Fourth, and equally crucial, we must plan for the development of others. Individuals will develop deep and broad commitments to organizations that focus on their continual growth and improvement. In an age of the knowledge worker, such planning is critical if individuals are to remain loyal to our organization.

A corollary of committing ourselves to the development of others is the recognition that we must focus on the strengths of our work associates, making their strengths effective and their weaknesses irrelevant.[2] When we fail to adopt this approach, we initiate a period of stagnation and decline that will eventually threaten the very vitality of the organization. In fact, the first sign of an organization's decline is the loss of its appeal to qualified, able and ambitious people.

The following five commitments motivate individuals to engage in productive contribution and ongoing development.

- A clear mission so that an individual can see how his or her contribution fits into the collective whole
- The careful placement of each individual into a job that maximizes strengths and minimizes weaknesses
- Opportunities for learning and improving that makes perpetual development possible and desirable
- High demands that require our best effort
- Consistent, predictable accountability in order to achieve results

Upon reviewing these five principles, we might easily assume that all individuals should be managed the same way. Yet, though these five principles are essential, this does not mean that we all should be managed the same. Drawing on Douglas McGregor's work *The Human Side of Enterprise*,[3] Drucker demonstrates that both he and McGregor initially got it wrong. By contrast, Maslow got it right with his emphasis that different people have to be managed differently.

The role of the effective leader is to give knowledge workers the guidance they need to make the contributions they are being asked to make. Once a leader establishes the standards, values, expected performance and required results, workers then understand clearly what contributions they will have to make. Yet they may select the fashion in which to make them. In other words, the effective leader doesn't worry about control of the process; rather, the effective leader focuses primarily on results.[4]

This focus informs the way an effective leader stays connected to his or her knowledge workers: by persuading them, rather than commanding them, to perform. Commitment to the principle of management by objectives allows an organization to build a true team and integrate individual efforts into a common achievement. Each member of the organization contributes something different, but all members must contribute toward a common goal.

Management by objectives and managing the knowledge worker as a partner rather than an employee are two qualities that reflect our commitment as a leader to hire competent people and then turn them loose to work. The commitment to viewing individual knowledge workers as partners is based not on emotionally laden experience but rather on the belief that this commitment evokes the best performance from all our work associates. Because of this commitment, four basic guidelines should direct our personnel decisions.[5]

First, if we select people for jobs in which they aren't good fits, we must reassign them so that they can make the contributions they are best able to make. I have believed this principle my entire life, but until I studied with Drucker, I had never heard anyone who was willing to lead this way. Every other situation in my experience had involved blame being placed exclusively on the malfunctioning employee, never on the ineffective boss.

Second, every knowledge worker has the right to competent command. This guideline maintains mutual respect, which makes joint performance possible and keeps morale high. This second principle must be combined with the first: that is, we have to have the right people in the right positions in order to fulfill our obligation to provide competent command. Still, despite our best efforts, we can end up with problem employees. Be mindful of providing competent command, but when an individual or department undermines the effectiveness of a competent leader, we have a renegade employee or department, not an incompetent manager.

Third, we all must recognize that our people decisions fundamentally determine the performance capacity of our organization. No matter how much we like someone, if he or she does not possess the competencies to perform well, hiring or retaining that person will harm the organization and ultimately compromise our effectiveness as a leader. Many well-meaning but undifferentiated leaders find this guideline problematic: they like individuals or groups, but are emotionally connected to them in ways that don't lead to effective results. Separating ourselves emotionally from our preference for an individual or group in order to provide competent command is of paramount importance.

Finally, we should only give new assignments with significant risks to people we know, people we have confidence in and whose judgment we trust. Throughout my career I have had to make many personnel decisions. Often the solution is obvious. However, when facing how to fill a position that has turned into a widow maker (in Drucker's terms, defeating two or more good people in a row), I have always reached out to an individual I know, I have confidence in and I trust. My rationale: I know if this individual fails, the failure is a result of deeper issues within the organization and not capacity issues on his or her part.

Drucker has emphasized that developing talent is critically important for the enduring success of any organization. Such development is only possible when senior leadership works to understand and guide the emerging class of new knowledge workers. More than any prior generation, this group feels the need for connection with leaders in their organizations and for those leaders' provision of opportunities to find meaning through their work.

An early pioneer in articulating the theoretical base for this philosophy of leadership is Jean Lipman-Blumen, a professor of management and a former colleague of Drucker's in the Drucker Center. Lipman-Blumen has developed a theory of "connective leadership," balancing the tension between excellence in individual contribution with the necessity of excellence in executive leadership.

This model of leadership was developed over a twenty-year period and reflects research she conducted with more than thirty-nine thousand people.[6] To guide her research she developed three quantitative instruments with Harold Leavitt, her Stanford colleague.[7] Out of this research, she identified three key sets of qualities each with three key sets of styles.[8]

"Connective leadership" contributes by helping us integrate our personal style with the organizational culture and environmental context in such a way that the alignment leads to great results. What I have found particularly compelling in Lipman-Blumen's work is how she elevates the human dimension in leadership: we must understand both individual and corporate contexts in order to lead well. This understanding highlights the critical importance of maintaining our convictions as leaders while maintaining our connections with work associates.

Leaders often start out with one of two biases: either imposing our will on organizations because we have vision without a connection to reality or capitulating our leadership responsibility and achieving nothing because we are co-opted into the status quo by our organizations. In the past four years I have learned the necessity of this dual focus from Robert J. Emmons, retired chairman and CEO of Smart & Final, and past professor of international marketing at the University of Southern California. Emmons embodies the principles of "connective leadership," and I have learned so much from him as we have discussed leadership effectiveness in the twenty-first century.

Achieving Great Results While Valuing Our Work Associates

I have had the privilege of interacting with Emmons on a frequent basis for the past four years. He is the retired chair and CEO of Smart & Final, an international chain of warehouse retail outlets, patterned after Costco and Walmart but using a smaller footprint and locating in older, more established urban centers. Our topics of conversation range from world affairs to poetry, leadership, the role of government in society, the necessity of morality and much more. Emmons is one of the most positive and optimistic individuals I've ever met; yet he displays the gritty toughness of a Detroit childhood.

Emmons is a living example of connective leadership. He popularized the notion of raising up a whole generation of "we" leaders; emphasizing that only great organizations are led by "we" leaders. When he spoke in my class recently, he began by noting a recent speech he had heard by a prominent politician in our country. While campaigning, this individual focused on being a "we" leader, but now, after two years in office, the politician had become almost single-minded in emphasizing "my" accomplishments, what "I" have done, and how these policies have affected "me." In contrast, great connective leaders always focus on the greater good and play the key role in raising the vision and sights of their associates.

Emmons also emphasizes that tomorrow's leaders will hold power not because of position but because of talent and respect. Leaders are no longer given a blank check of confidence and appreciation. The multiple scandals over the past several years have destroyed our confidence in the honesty and integrity that was the bedrock of corporate America. As a result of this moral decline, higher scrutiny is inevitable. In fact, Emmons argues that only through this scrutiny will we be able to recover the respect that is so critical for effective leadership.

This scrutiny will also impact loyalty. Fifty years ago a company could count on employee loyalty. With the emergence of the knowledge worker and the erosion of lifetime employment, employees no longer anticipate or even plan to stay at one job for an entire career. In fact, according to Emmons, employees are viewed as lacking ambition if they don't move on every few years. The goal, then, is to create the sort of culture, atmosphere and connectedness that makes employees want to stay long term.

At the heart of employee respect is a leader's capacity to generate vision and execute strategy. At the heart of each leader's vision and strategy are the knowledge workers who carry it out. As Emmons once wrote, "relationships drive success."[9] Relationships and our ability to connect with key constituents, in fact, drive all other aspects of the organization. Relationships with customers, suppliers, service consultants and even company associates determine the level of success an organization enjoys.

As a result, human resources remain the most important resource of every organization. In order to maximize opportunities for the future, moreover, every organization will have to capitalize on the broad and diverse pool of talent that constitutes its work force. This broad pool of talent will bring with it unique challenges that cannot be ignored. For instance, integrating individuals from diverse backgrounds will require deliberate, consistent effort.

During his own time as a CEO, Emmons developed an in-house training program titled "Smart University." This training institute allowed all employees to progress in workplace development as well as to undergo continuous training and improvement that made them more efficient in their work. It also allowed Emmons and the entire Smart & Final management team to instill the organizational culture that carried the company through major transitions within its industry.

Recently, when Emmons spoke in class, he emphasized that the most effective leaders always begin and end with fundamental respect for their work associates. Humility teaches a leader to respect the knowledge and expertise that every member of the organization brings to work every day.

This baseline of respect makes it possible to develop and maintain the type of connection that allows leadership and influence to flow freely within the organization. Such leadership and influence, in turn, provide the effective leader with the platform from which to cast vision and deploy strategy. As a result, Emmons implemented multiple strategies to ensure that the culture of Smart & Final would be a welcoming place for his work associates.

These strategies included the launch of an annual family picnic so that everyone could gather to experience the personal lives and families of work associates. He launched programs that helped every member of the company discover his or her role in the overall work of the company. His "I Make a Difference" campaign expressed the human longing to make a contribution that will make a difference. Emmons leveraged human motivation, which catapults a company to remarkable results.

His leadership was not without controversy. Confronting a union culture that discouraged cooperation between labor and management (e.g., challenging participation in company events based on union or nonunion status), Emmons worked to bridge these differences and improve relationships. Some of his gestures, like having the names of each driver placed on the side panels of his or her delivery truck, seemed small. However, the results spoke for themselves: productivity soared while maintenance costs plummeted. Emmons's key to success was communicating the fundamental values of integrity, care and respect. Emmons believes that people matter, and his work associates knew it. We have to communicate the value of people in ways that matter to them, not just ways that matter to us.

Emmons believes our language use and word choice matter. He stopped referring to the workers as *employees;* instead, he began calling them *associates.* He also insisted that conversations maintain a civil tone. Again, these may seem like small gestures, but his attention to the ways that corporate language shapes institutional culture has been remarkable. This language sensitivity, in turn, helped engineer a transition at Smart & Final from employees seeing their contributions as an individual matter to seeing their contributions as accomplishments of the team.

Ultimately, the launch of Smart University helped lower the

fear and anxiety of Emmons's work associates. A common mistake for many companies when launching a change initiative is forgetting about the anxiety this sets off within current associates. By launching Smart University, Emmons demonstrated that the company was committed to every employee, including long-serving employees. This commitment to employee training signaled that the company would give every associate the opportunity to grow and develop in order to continue being a productive, contributing member of the team.

The results were staggering in terms of success. By the time Emmons retired, Smart University was offering eighty courses and teaching the principles of management across all levels of the company. It had also garnered the interest and support of others in the food industry—including Trader Joe's, which outsourced its employee training to Smart & Final. This emphasis on corporate culture, moreover, demonstrated the priority Emmons had placed on it. The desire to create a culture of integrity, care and respect reflected Emmons's priority as an involved, connected leader. By being committed to helping individuals become all that they could be, Emmons ensured the long-term loyalty and success of his company.

Today, we know that the way forward will require us to manage in collaborative environments. The outdated and timeworn approaches of command and control will not secure the level of talent that is necessary for long-term, sustainable success. Knowledge workers simply won't put up with an atmosphere that is repressive of their contribution and reactive to their input.

Working in a college environment, I am surrounded by knowledge workers. What I have experienced in this environment is that everyone desires a culture of integrity, care and respect. They do not need to know everything, but they want appropriate levels of honesty and transparency so they may understand what is happening in all facets of the college. They also want to have appropriate levels of input without needing to dominate. As a result, we have been able to develop a level of participatory management because our roles are understood, our mission is clear and our strategy is compelling.

Ultimately, we come to work each day because we believe we are contributing to something that will outlive us. Nothing is more compelling than making an ultimate contribution to purposes that are greater than ourselves.[10]

The Quest for Character: Indifference Versus Diligence

Indifference and impatient discouragement result from believing that the current investment of our lives does not matter. These negative attitudes reflect a perception that what we are currently doing has no enduring value. Drucker recognized this dynamic and spoke about the need either to find new work or find a second volunteer career where we could find meaning. As many of us enter midlife, we may experience being overlooked for promotions or perhaps experience other major setbacks in our career. Often, these experiences make us lose heart. In fact, they can even trigger major bouts of depression. Or the trigger may not be a setback at all, but simply boredom from doing the same thing over and over, year in and year out. It is in these challenging moments that we can find our greatest joy by becoming engaged in activities that bring joy and happiness to others.

In contrast, diligence strengthens our resolve and helps us persevere through these tough times, knowing that our contributions make a difference. Every one of us either is facing or will face situations and circumstances that test us. Our ability to endure these trials and come through them in a way that keeps our leadership intact will give us even greater platforms from which to influence the direction of organizations. Of course, our ability to endure is often tied to the level of confidence and commitment we feel to the organization we are leading.

When we persevere, we discover a depth of meaning and purpose that is never obvious at first glance. Indifference is a result of not seeing the deeper meaning to our present work. Diligence is the character trait that arises when our immediate work is tough and there is no clear end to our challenges in sight, but we carry on believing that the outcome in the future will be worth all the present difficulties we face.

In my own life as a leader, I have gone through periods of intense scrutiny and challenge. In every case, the sense of the greater good being accomplished by the organization kept me from quitting. In fact, in every case, the mission of the organization always exceeded the inconvenience of the task. Ultimately, facing hardships and challenges is part of leadership; persevering through them will shape us in ways so unique that we are forever changed, and our organization will be better off because we endured.

Principle 8

MAKING AN ULTIMATE CONTRIBUTION

Discovering Life's Greatest Purpose

The final requirement of effective leadership is to earn trust. Trust is the conviction that the leader means what he says. It is a belief in something very old-fashioned called "integrity." A leader's actions and a leader's professed beliefs must be congruent, or at least compatible. Effective leadership is not based on being clever; it is based primarily on being consistent. It is through trust that we lift a person's vision to higher sights and ask and answer, "What do you want to be remembered for?"

Peter Drucker

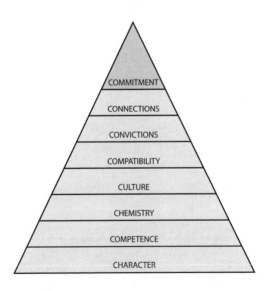

"Eventually, you have to give back." These words still linger in my mind. Peter Drucker stated them as we were wrapping up our first lunch. His sense of making an ultimate contribution guided him, and he hoped it would guide me. Woody Allen once joked that he wanted to gain immortality not by his work but by not dying. Oh, to be so lucky. Since we all face death, it is left to us to determine how we will live and how we give our lives and our leadership to purposes that will outlive us. In this way, we gain a sense of the immortality we crave by the contributions we make to the lives of others and to the institutions and organizations that will continue long after we are gone.

In *Good to Great*, Jim Collins writes that great leaders sublimate their own ego in order to serve the greater good of their organization. This orientation is the hallmark of their success. In pursuing this commitment, Collins notes, leaders invest their life energies in purposes that will outlive them. In other words, they make an ultimate contribution.

In *Management Challenges for the 21st Century*,[1] Drucker identifies the essence of making an ultimate contribution as the quest for meaning. He also notes that the great challenge to making this ultimate contribution often strikes before we are ready, and is the hallmark of a midlife crisis resulting from boredom.

Work, meaningful as it may be, can lose its appeal. Red Poling once remarked that as he ended his career he grew less and less interested in the problems and more and more interested in the people. The demanding side of work can escalate until work no longer provides the challenges that captivate the minds and imaginations of effective leaders. Eventually, they begin to look for something more. In this quest they seek opportunities that will bring meaning. They have made their money; now they want their lives to count, to make an impact, to really matter.

Drucker advocated developing a second interest long before we exhaust our first interest. This parallel career becomes not only our lifeblood for meaningful work and service opportunities in the future, but also a source of great support if we were to experience major setbacks in the present. But how do we make this move?

All of us make this move when a trusted mentor shows us the way. Long before Drucker expanded my understanding of this principle, I first learned it from my father, Richard Beebe, who often spoke to me about his own quest for meaning.

Developing a Second Interest While Living with Purpose

My father died on September 12, 1989, from massive complications triggered by cardiac arrest. He was sixty. We were shocked. He walked two to four miles every day, had grown up on a farm and had regular checkups. His own father lived to eighty-eight, his oldest brother turned ninety this year, and all of his siblings have lived well into their eighties. The stress of his job as a public school superintendent and earlier periods of inactivity had taken their toll. Now he was dead.

I was thirty when it happened. I spoke with him once a week, had visited with him on the morning of his cardiac arrest and considered him to be my key mentor. Even now I find myself remembering conversations and comments he made more than twenty years ago. I had enjoyed growing up with him as my father, but I had especially enjoyed entering adulthood—a time when we were able to share problems, seek advice and enjoy the friendship that comes with maturity.

Subsequent to his death, I was contacted by Dennis Hagen, who had completed an administrative internship with my father for a class at the University of Oregon. The internship had focused on the responsibilities and priorities of being a successful public school superintendent. It included different observations of daily responsibilities. It also included long conversations about what motivates a person to engage in this type of career.[2]

My father believed his first responsibility was to be the chief motivator of quality education. He sought to motivate in two primary ways: by being physically present at all types of public events in order to offer his full and visible support for the complete range of the school district's activities, and by building a strong image for the school district through positive reporting that focused on each student being given the opportunity to maximize his or her potential.

More than anything, my father demonstrated a unique capacity to be emotionally present with other people. He showed this capacity with his family as well as the people he worked with and served. An effective leader learns how to be emotionally present; my father often said, "Wherever you are, be there." He meant to convey that we should learn to live each moment so that the people we are with feel the full impact of our presence.

While providing quality education to a community was his first priority, he also contributed to the quality of life of the entire community. Whether promoting area centennials or working with state government to improve the safety of nearby roads, he believed he was responsible to make a positive contribution in all areas of life.

Essentially, he had a bias for action and believed that his responsibility as an effective leader was to look at what a situation required and do it. He had little regard for prima donnas, for the individuals in an organization who believe the organization exists to serve their ego needs. Instead, he focused on what each individual could do to serve the greater good. This focus could not be captured by a job description. No job description adequately conveys the sense that some of the responsibilities of an effective leader are looking around and then getting involved in solving problems that will fundamentally improve the lives of those he or she serves.

My father also worked to create a positive atmosphere in all aspects of the organization, including his interaction with the board and the general public. Throughout our conversations, he often punctuated his remarks with illustrations of how situations turned into disasters when people settled private matters in a public way. He felt that solving private matters in a public way not only caused a specific situation to escalate, thereby taking too much time with too little success, but also caused the entire organization to lose track of its mission. Conversely, by handling private matters privately, the school district was able to focus its public energy and attention on providing quality education for all its students.

My father worked in the same school district for thirty years. Prior to becoming superintendent, he worked for some great bosses and for some not-so-great bosses. His basic orientation was to speak well when he could and to not speak at all when he couldn't say something positive. You often had to listen for his silence.

Dad also enjoyed drawing upon his early upbringing on an Eastern Oregon farm. My grandparents homesteaded a farm during the Great Depression. Many of my dad's formative years were spent working with and learning from animals. This farm wisdom guided him his entire life. He wondered out loud about the value of rattlesnakes, often musing that bull snakes did the exact same thing without doing any harm to humans. He loved horses and felt an exhilarating freedom when he rode them. As a teenager his favorite form of work was entering the box canyons of Eastern Oregon, capturing wild horses and breaking them in so he could sell them to area ranchers.

From these and other experiences, he learned to do no harm and to sense the individual spirit of every creature. He also learned a wisdom and orientation to life that he shared readily. Many of these sayings were not original with him: he was always picking up pieces of wisdom along the way. What was original was his ability to speak the right word at the right moment in the right way. This uncanny gift of discernment gave him a moral authority that brought influence; it also brought responsibility.

When cautioning me about getting drawn into no-win arguments, he would say, "It's like wrestling with a pig—you both get dirty and the pig loves it." When helping me learn how to assess criticism, he would suggest, "If one man calls you a donkey, you can ignore it, but if five do, you'd better buy a saddle." When teaching me how to keep my balance despite what life brings, he would state, "Never let success corrupt you or failure define you." When encouraging me to do my best and stay focused on my responsibilities, he would offer, "The only two things in life you can control are attitude and effort."

He believed an effective leader had to maintain his or her moral compass. His own moral instruction often came through indirect communication. More often than not, he would recall a story from his past or an incident we had observed together and then share his observations without preaching or putting others down.

Regarding the evils of gambling, he would cite the misfortune of an elderly man we often saw when visiting my grandparents. Earlier in life he had lost his entire farm while gambling, thereby throwing a whole family onto the welfare of the community. Regarding the need to honor my word and do what I said I would do, he would cite a careless neighbor who lived with "situational integrity," which my father defined as follows: "He means well in the moment; he just can't sustain his commitments over time."

He believed every one of us has been given unique gifts and abilities and that, as an educator, it was his responsibility to maximize this potential. He loved to see other people succeed: he never felt threatened by the success of others, and he taught us to celebrate their success as well.

He also believed we should be open to learning from anyone. Listen attentively. Show proper respect. Remember that insight could come from any corner.

His school district included conservative Christians and left-over hippies. This created an interesting tension. One week he would have some parents protesting the use of *Catcher in the Rye* or *Lord of the Flies*. The next week he would have other parents missing altogether while law enforcement officials raided their now defunct pot farms. Still, the context defined the contribution. In every case my father's emphasis was that the effective leader worked for the greater good of the community, and especially the greater good of the students of that community. This commitment required him to love and serve the people in his path. Ultimately, he believed that we should always strive to do our best, we should always remember the people who invested in us, and we should always give back.

In fact, it was this sense both of duty and responsibility that drove him. Throughout his adult life he balanced his responsibilities at work with his keen interest in the college we had all attended and in active participation in our local and regional church. These were his "second" interests, where he found so much meaning and purpose. What I learned from my father is that my first responsibility, my first interest, is where I make my living. Here, I have the opportunity to learn how to work and to bring a quality of leadership that is positive and restorative.

My second interest, moreover, allows the principles, priorities and life lessons I have learned in my first interest to inform my other work. One of Drucker's great points in developing a second interest was the buffer it created between disappointment at work and the need we have as humans to make a positive contribution that matters. In the last year of my father's shortened life, he retired from a major volunteer position that had brought great joy and meaning to him. A mere month before his passing, he gave his last public address as he was being honored for his work. Lost in the chaos that would ensue a month later was his thankfulness for being able to make a contribution to an organization that had mattered so much to him. In his address, he summarized that we all need to be part of something greater than ourselves, and we all need to have opportunities to give back.

I could have learned these lessons from anyone. Fortunately, I was able to learn them from my father. My father gave me a learning orientation that has influenced my entire life: he taught me to be open to the input of others. Like so many individuals in my life, including those cited throughout this book, when we have a disposition to learn from anyone, life can be a great teacher. Life is filled with incredible individuals willing to share the wisdom they have gained along the way. Be open to the influence of others. Be teachable. Live life with a spirit of integrity, care and respect. In this way, you will have the opportunity to make a contribution that will outlive you.

As long as we are willing to lead, we need mentors. We never outgrow our need for the input of trusted associates who can provide perspective. One of the great joys of leading an organization is forming friendships as we learn to lean on others. These trusted advisers help us understand our circumstances and provide insight that strengthens our understanding. To lead effectively, we need to seek out the company of those who will inspire, encourage and hold us accountable to our highest ideals.

The Quest for Character: Melancholy Versus Wisdom

The final character challenge is melancholy. Melancholy is treacherous. It results from a sense that both our current contribution and our entire existence have not mattered. This deadly thought indicates a complete loss of confidence that the world will remember us or that our contribution to life will have any lingering effect after we are gone. Often manifest in feeling that our desires have been thwarted, melancholy can emerge from unbridled anger that people no longer give us what we believe to be our proper dues. It often results if the deadly thought of envy remains unresolved. In my own line of work I often see melancholy in those who have never developed an identity beyond their own work. The need for the acclaim of others and the fear that their contributions will somehow be forgotten causes them to slump into depression or to lash out in anger and pride.

Wisdom, on the other hand, is the ability to recognize the role our lives play in the greater affairs of the world at the same time as we learn to let go. Wisdom is finding contentment with our individual contributions and recognizing that the roles we have played will affect the next generation as we release our leadership responsibilities to those who follow us. It is learning to enjoy our legacy without needing to tidy it up before we are gone.

Finis

WHEN OUR TIME IS UP

Making Sure Our Life Has Mattered

Eventually, the clock runs out. Whether our time ends suddenly, as it did for my father, or it erodes over time, as it did for Peter Drucker, every one of us comes to the end. What then will be our contribution? Aristotle once observed that we cannot say whether a person has lived well or poorly until he or she is dead and we assess the entire breadth of his or her life experience. In order to inform the life investments we are currently making, then, we should reflect on what each of us wants our ultimate contribution to be.

Robert Greenleaf once remarked, "The leadership crisis in America is without precedent." This observation was made more than twenty-five years ago, and the situation has only worsened. Sadly, many today who once aspired to leadership have simply given up. Vast numbers of well-intentioned leaders have exhausted themselves yet have little to show for it.

Others have undermined their contribution by believing multiple experiences would strengthen their leadership. Their penchant for moving on has allowed them to avoid facing the consequences of their decisions. It has also restricted their development.

Instead of having twenty-five years of experience, they have twenty-five one-year experiences. They have changed responsibilities so often that they have failed to undergo the development that comes from facing mistakes.

Still others have committed career-limiting mistakes: chasing after instant results, being careless in their people decisions or simply making moral compromises that are the deadly sin of their industry. The siren song of instant results is hard to ignore. In a celebrity culture like ours, we expect the successful leader to make a big impact and to make it almost instantly.

And then there is a leadership malaise that touches us all to one extent or another. I am referring to how completely we have become accustomed to the normality of dysfunctional leadership. The constant media stream of scandals and wrongdoing have calloused us to these human and organizational catastrophes, and the toll they exact on our society. This overall leadership dysfunction is so pervasive in our culture that it is nearly impossible for us to have a clear vision of the necessity and importance of effective leadership.

Longing for Effective Leaders

And yet there is a great cadre of leaders in all walks of life who help us see the significance and importance of effective leadership. They have found that the pursuit of excellence and the capacity for leadership have allowed them to make contributions that will outlive them.

All the individuals I have featured in this book entered into the various responsibilities of leadership so their lives would make a difference. I have described these various approaches as "the eight essential principles of effective leadership":

- the necessity of character
- the importance of competence

- the advantage of team chemistry
- the interplay of culture and context
- the strength of compatibility and coherence
- the guidance of convictions
- the significance of maintaining our connections
- the opportunity to make an ultimate contribution

These principles do not operate separately from one another. Indeed, they build on each other, and their effect is cumulative.

In the final analysis, do you have the longing to be a leader? The world desperately needs individuals willing to pay the price, undergo the development process and put up with the inconvenience in order to provide effective leadership. It doesn't really matter where you find yourself today. If you have a longing to make a difference through your leadership, begin where you are and get underway. Strive to make progress every day. This longing and striving will provide the motivation you need to improve. They will stimulate you to accept more and more responsibility. Ultimately, they will give you the opportunity to make a difference through your life.

ACKNOWLEDGMENTS

Every book is a community effort. These ideas were initially developed as I made several presentations on leadership and as I was teaching different classes on leadership. I am especially grateful to have presented these ideas to different sections of the EB150: Seminar in Executive Leadership class at Westmont College.

I am indebted to each person featured in this book. Peter Drucker is my main source, and I remain forever grateful that Roger Minthorne encouraged me to pursue the dual degree at Claremont Graduate University so that I could study with Drucker. Each of the other individuals has played a key role in my life as well. So my thanks go out to Diogenes Allen, Stuart Professor of Philosophy at Princeton Theological Seminary (emeritus), who gave me so many of the intellectual and moral anchors that have sustained me; to Richard J. Foster, my long-time friend, colleague and coauthor, whose life and thought have done so much to shape my own; to Steve Sample, who was so gracious and helpful as I began my career as a college president and has always made a place for me; to Harold A. "Red" Poling, who turned once-a-month lunches at the Ritz-Carlton into a learning laboratory that will last a lifetime; to Alvin Roberts, who made a summer of Thursdays so memorable and whose wisdom and guidance are with me to this day; to John Beckett, who taught me the principles of hiring for mission and the gift and grace of enduring friendship; to Dave McKenna, who, after my father died, became a spiritual and professional mentor unlike any other; to Robert Emmons, who always makes the circle bigger and has taught me so much about living life with integrity, care and respect; and to the memory of my father, Richard H. Beebe. May we all be blessed to have a father who loves his own and cares about the character and contribution of his children.

I also want to thank Nancy Town, my executive assistant, who has provided able assistance throughout this entire project. Special thanks to Vince Nelson, Les Dietzman and Rick Ifland, who read portions of the book in manuscript form and provided encouragement and support throughout the whole project. Rick Wallace, professor of organizational management at Spring Arbor University, and Dave Newton, professor of entrepreneurial finance at Westmont College, have been gracious in letting me co-teach with them as these ideas were taking shape. Sam Riggleman, athletic director and head baseball coach at Spring Arbor, still has the napkin where I first charted out the pyramid. Special thanks to Deborah Dunn, professor of communication studies, Westmont College, who was especially helpful on chapter four. Bob Fryling, publisher, and Cindy Bunch, senior editor, at InterVarsity Press, have believed in this project from the beginning and I'm grateful. Cindy was unusually helpful as she provided remarkable guidance as I worked my way to a final manuscript. Thanks, indeed.

I especially want to acknowledge the wonderful contributions of Kirby Ifland. Kirby was my research assistant for this entire project. He is a recent graduate of Westmont College, a remarkably gifted young man, and already underway at Harvard Law School, preparing to make a difference as a lawyer. Kirby attended a semester of classes so he could hear the principles live and has read every draft of the manuscript. His contributions on every front have made this project better.

Finally, I want to thank my family. My wife, Pam, has watched these ideas unfold throughout the twenty-two years of our married life and has often been the conversation partner as I was thinking through how best to approach this book. Our oldest daughter, Anna, is a budding author and an able critic. She too read the entire manuscript and offered helpful suggestions, alternative word choices and better sentence structures, all of which helped to strengthen the final product. Our second daughter, Elizabeth, and our son, Richard, have read various portions and have asked probing questions that helped me think through how I could present these ideas better. Ultimately, I am thankful for their love and encouragement that makes all I do in life richer, fuller and more enjoyable.

APPENDIX 1

An Overview of Top Management Work
in the Twentieth Century

Writers and scholars in the first half of the twentieth century depicted the CEO as a larger-than-life persona taking charge of all activities of the organization in order to ensure adequate performance by the company.[1] Later thinkers extended the CEO's importance, placing particular stress on the role of the chief executive in spearheading strategic planning, refining and articulating institutional missions and goals, and balancing the needs and competencies of the organizations with the development and contribution of its people.[2]

Following World War II, a proliferation of books attempted to define the emerging role of leadership in the modern world. These efforts culminated in Henry Mintzberg's landmark study in which Mintzberg defined a set of ten managerial roles distributed among three broad categories: interpersonal (figurehead, leader and liaison), informational (monitor, disseminator and spokesperson), and decisional (entrepreneur, disturbance handler, resource allocator and negotiator).[3]

Many other studies either expand or condense Mintzberg's categories,[4] but all pale in comparison to Sydney Finkelstein's *Strategic Leadership*, the landmark study published in 2009.[5] Finkelstein's work is a tour de force of the entire range of writing on leadership and management over the past one hundred years. He summarizes the basic dimensions of the job of executive leadership into three broad categories and provides both key insights about the nature of current leadership and provocative observations about necessary research for the future.

Finkelstein, like Drucker, dismisses the naysayers from the 1960s and 1970s who questioned the validity of the CEO. For both men, the CEO is not only important to the overall success of the organization, he or she as CEO is the one person on whom the fortunes of the organization rise or fall. Finkelstein also emphasizes the role top executives play in allocating resources, establishing and enforcing policies, and developing an organization that is aligned strategically. All of these priorities highlight the role of the chief executive in being responsible for performance.

Finkelstein's reflections and consolidations of one hundred years of research are profound. Here, Finkelstein captures the earlier insights of Isaac Ansoff who had emphasized the central role of the CEO in establishing and executing strategy.[6] Ultimately, Finkelstein concludes this important section by highlighting the role of substance and symbols. Executives cannot help but act symbolically. Whether intentional or accidental, the behavior of top executives establishes the boundaries of corporate behavior and the priorities or preferences of the company.[7]

An interesting challenge of Finkelstein's study, however, is that while it provides the most comprehensive assessment of leadership over the past one hundred years, it does little to lay out an actual game plan for how to develop into an effective leader. This is why Drucker is so important. Drucker has the rare ability to teach us how to think like an executive, how to engage in a thought process that helps us answer difficult and complex questions in order to determine the direction and destiny of our organization. In this way Drucker helps us understand how to execute our chief responsibilities while ascertaining and applying our core competencies.

Contemporary Sources on Top Management Teams

Interest in the study of top management teams has exploded in recent years. There are several reasons for this development. First, top management teams represent different areas within the organization that often compete with one another for scarce resources. This competition can benefit the organization, but it can also be highly disruptive and keep an organization from achieving its ultimate goals by fragmenting its objectives.

Second, strategic decision making has become highly complex. This complexity is displayed in the stages, sequences and processes that a group of top managers undertake as they make decisions that shape the destiny of the company.[8] This interaction reflects the distribution of power and the decision processes that will guide the organization as it sets its long-term course.

Third, it has become increasingly obvious that no single person can run an organization. Several writers note that understanding the makeup and disposition of a top management team gives far greater predictive accuracy than studying the CEO alone.[9] As a result, scholars have developed a keen interest in the composition, structure and interaction patterns of top management teams.[10]

The composition of the team is based on the values, beliefs, personalities, backgrounds and biases of each of the individual members. When old members and new members are blended into a new team, these diverse backgrounds bring a richness of perspective that provides creative alternatives when making a decision.[11]

The structure of the team is defined by the roles each participant fills as well as the structure of responsibility that may already exist. For example, in higher education the provost or chief academic officer is always assumed to be the second in command. This inherent bias tilts all decision conversations in a certain direction.

Finally, the nature and pattern of group interaction is influenced most directly by the level of trust and mutual respect that each member of the team carries for one another. There are several writers who diminish the importance of trust and mutual respect, but I have found that people who do not like each other rarely trust each other, and people who do not trust each other often develop political behaviors that become counterproductive for the organization.[12] This recognition helps us see that strategic decisions are made by leaders who exist not in a vacuum but in a complex web of social and political relationships both within the organization and in the broader environmental context.

Within the environmental context three factors are especially important.[13] First, the complexity of the environment directly influences the level of tolerance within the executive team and the degree to which a variety of solutions will be explored. In higher education, for example, the current environment is highly volatile as demographics shift, state and federal financial aid is substantially altered, and the entire country adjusts to the worldwide economic meltdown. These external factors have a direct bearing on our decision making and on the way we process information in making our decisions.

Second, the level of environmental instability has a direct bearing on the size, interdependence and capacity to reach consensus of the top management team. This instability can come from any number of areas, including changes in the competitive mix of our industry, regulatory changes imposed by governmental agencies, a crisis that affects the organization or a sudden change in the membership of the executive team due to departure or dismissal of one or more of its members. The impact of this instability can be disruptive, or it can be a time when the team comes together as it works through these challenges successfully.

Finally, it is essential that the CEO play a leading role in the shaping, priority setting and decision making of the team. Again, the past fifty years have been a period of immense interest and study, the result of which has been the conclusion that the CEO plays a pivotal role in at least three key areas. First, the CEO essentially determines how and what the group will address by controlling the agenda. Second, if the CEO has a strong vision for the organization and communicates this vision regularly and effectively, the members of the team begin to frame their plans within the larger landscape of this overarching vision. Finally, the extent to which the CEO has charisma will have a direct impact on the level of effort and commitment that members of the team are willing to exert.[14]

The capacity of the CEO is also highly important. A CEO's capacity is established by at least three key areas: a broad educational background, a breadth of work experiences and a disposition to take input from a variety of sources.[15] The quality and capacity of the CEO also has a direct bearing on the quality and capacity of the executive team.

In addition, the chief executive, as the central member of the team, determines who will be on the team. The level of openness, the level of comfort with disagreement and the level of tolerance of ideas and discussions that go beyond the CEO's own area of responsibility fundamentally shape the quality of team interaction and ultimately, the quality of strategic decisions. Conversely, if the CEO is not open to a variety of ideas and inputs, and instead insists on a narrow range of focus and discussion, the level of engagement will diminish and the quality and range of decisions will be reduced as well.[16]

APPENDIX 2

Robert Wuthnow's Eight Spheres of Society

Robert Wuthnow's landmark study, *Communities of Discourse,* identifies eight key spheres that shape and guide every society.

The first sphere is the *social setting,* which is constituted by two primary factors: environmental conditions and institutional structures. Environmental conditions include the impact of population changes due to birth, immigration or plague, as well as disruptions due to war or economic depression. Institutional factors include what is embedded and displaced within society. A primary concern is the way the government works to institutionalize the public and private values of the community.

The second sphere, *economics,* includes a review of the production capacities within the society, the selection processes by which goods and services are pursued or denied, and the way the society institutionalizes these decisions. Many of the most significant economic changes in world history are tied to rapid technological change.

Additional economic concerns include the management of scarce natural resources, the coordination of distribution channels and the capability to establish necessary plant capacities. Finally, economic concerns include the development of a central bank, the coordination of capital accumulation and distribution and the governance of money supply. The implosion of the world-wide economy in 2008 demonstrated how vulnerable we are to changes in the environmental context triggered by changes in the macroeconomic environment.

The third sphere, *the political dimension*, is concerned with the massive responsibility of integrating and maintaining a diverse population. Relevant documents from America's founding, including the Articles of Confederation, *The Federalist Papers* and the Bill of Rights, show their authors considering the complex question of how to integrate immigrants into the fabric of American life.[1] Additionally, the political system must coordinate fair and equitable taxation, establish institutions that support and reinforce self-governance, and answer and address issues concerned with the overall maintenance and stability of a society.

The fourth sphere, *the religious sphere*, focuses on how religion is institutionalized within a culture, including whether religion is a part of society or whether it is ostracized or even forbidden. The involvement the state plays in the regulation of religion—along with whether its context is urban, suburban or rural—is also considered significant. Additionally, the different religious expressions found in the use of text and liturgy either reinforce or clash with the prevailing culture. These practices in turn legitimate or undermine the credibility of religion in each society.

The fifth sphere is the way a culture *defines and responds to deviance*. Every social group suffers violation of its governing norms. The way this deviance is perceived and punished will reflect broader social forces at work than simply the individual deviant act itself. Was the deviant act primarily a religious, moral, political, legal or economic violation? Each of these elements play a role in how defiance is defined and handled.

The contributions of *art*, *education*, *entertainment* and *leisure* help determine and articulate the cultural values that make up the sixth sphere. The ways that cultural change occurs (in an abrupt or gradual fashion) and how these disruptions are perceived (as being progressive or repressive) are essential elements. Societies construct their interpretive frameworks and collective commitments in unique ways. These frameworks that provide meaning help societies when they are in the midst of upheaval and change.

The seventh sphere is the *role of the military and the police*. Of particular concern is what role the military plays in the implementation of state policy, along with what role the military plays as economic expansion takes an individual country's concerns beyond its national borders.

The eighth sphere is the way that *the judicial and legal institutions of a society are coordinated and supervised*. Of particular importance are factors such as whether or not citizens enjoy autonomy from state control, the rationalization of formal law, and the interpretation and application of their constitution and defining documents.

NOTES

Preface

[1]Peter Drucker, *The Effective Executive* (San Francisco: Harper & Row, 1966).

[2]I would finish the course work for my MBA in the fall of 1993 and have the degree posted on January 17, 1994. I had finished the course work for my Ph.D. that previous summer, but at Claremont your MA is posted after you successfully complete your comprehensive exams. I would finish my comprehensive exams and have my MA posted in 1995 and then finish my dissertation and have my Ph.D. posted in 1997.

[3]The four classes were Management of People at Work, Management and Society, The Effective Decision, and Management of International Business. Peter always taught on Monday afternoons, from 1-4 p.m., without breaks. All four classes were in Albrecht Auditorium, the tiered, horseshoe-shaped room on campus especially suited for the case-study approach to teaching, which he preferred.

[4]For example, his claim that all college campuses would become obsolete misses the point that college is about more than just completing a curriculum. Or his outlandish claims that it doesn't matter if members of an executive team get along; they should only be defined by their results. This emphasis misses the point that we have to have a certain level of camaraderie to sustain an executive team capable of achieving long-term results.

Principle 1: The Necessity of Character

[1]Plato, *The Dialogues: Meno*, trans. R. E. Allen (New Haven, Conn.: Yale University Press, 1984).

[2]Lawrence Kohlberg, *Theories of Moral Reasoning* (Cambridge, Mass.: Harvard University Press, 1980).

[3]Peter Drucker, *Management: Tasks, Responsibilities, Practices* (New York: Harper & Row, 1973), p. 462.

[4]Ibid.

[5]Ibid.

[6]Ibid., p. 402.

[7]Ibid., p. 463.

[8]Ibid., p. 456.

[9]Erik Erikson, *Childhood and Society* (New York: Norton, 1950).

[10]Peter Drucker, *The Essential Drucker* (New York: HarperCollins, 2001), p. 271.

[11]The chart is meant to provide an adequate treatment of the vices and virtues and their corresponding application to each level of the pyramid.

[12]Benedict, *The Rule of St. Benedict*. These qualities are the modifications of the ones

St. Benedict identifies for choosing a leader.

[13]Developing these character qualities is essential. Since we are not born with these qualities, we must engage in specific disciplines in order that they develop. The following list of ten life-giving disciplines are self-explanatory, and when practiced usher us into the sort of moral reflection that leads to growth and maturity: (1) Recognize the need for regular times of uninterrupted thinking and reflecting. (2) Be willing to engage in professional development activities that help us become self-aware, understanding what motivates us, what repulses us and what gives us the greatest sense of accomplishment. (3) Engage in regular intake of relevant information through reading and conferences, remembering that the average reader can complete twenty-four books a year and over seven hundred books during a thirty-year career. (4) Cultivate a capacity for empathy that helps us understand the needs and aspirations of others. A beautiful illustration of this principle is found in Max DePree's classic *Leadership Is an Art*. (5) Develop a proper attitude of respect for those in authority over us. This respect sets the tone and example for the way the rest of the organization will respond to authority. (6) Become open to the input of trusted friends. (7) Learn to hold confidences and engage in appropriate levels of honesty and transparency by being fair and discerning in all circumstances. (8) Be faithful and true to our word. (9) Avoid career-limiting mistakes by learning to value the norms and practices of our organizations. (10) Be disciplined and stay on track. "If you don't know where you're going, then any path will get you there."

Principle 2: The Importance of Competence

[1]Peter Drucker, *The Essential Drucker* (New York: HarperCollins, 2001), chap. 13.

[2]Peter Drucker, *Management: Tasks, Responsibilities, Practices* (New York: Harper & Row, 1973), chap. 33.

[3]In teaching and lecturing, Drucker assumed the basic components of business management were being met. The core curriculum of the MBA program at Claremont is fairly consistent with the curriculum in all leading MBA programs.

[4]Drucker, *Management*, chap. 49.

[5]Drucker, *Essential Drucker*, chap. 2.

[6]Peter F. Drucker, *Classic Drucker: Essential Wisdom from Peter Drucker from the Pages of "Harvard Business Review"* (Boston: Harvard Business Review, 2006), chap. 14. Also Peter Drucker, *The New Realities* (New York: Harper & Row, 1989), chap. 15.

[7]Drucker, *Essential Drucker*, chap. 6.

[8]Ibid.

[9]Peter F. Drucker, *The Effective Executive* (New York: Harper & Row, 1966). A single chapter from this original treatment is also in Drucker, *Classic Drucker*, chap. 9: "What Makes an Effective Executive," pp. 115-25.

[10]Drucker, *Management*, chap. 31.

[11]Ibid., chap. 50. To amplify and illustrate the importance of Peter's writings, let's first consider the context in which he did his most profound work. Among the twentieth century's great achievements stands the explosion of the development of large-scale

organizations and the need for effective leadership to guide them. Peter's life spanned this entire century, providing seminal guidance to our unfolding understanding of leadership. As organizations grew and the importance of senior management and especially the CEO became more evident, a multitude of studies helped define and refine our understanding of their unique work.

[12]See appendix 1 for a brief overview.

[13]Drucker, *Classic Drucker*, p. 94.

[14]Ibid., chap. 12.

[15]Drucker, *Management*, chap. 14.

[16]Ibid., chap. 16. First, humans have a *physiological* dimension. The body is not a machine, and work must be organized to respect the human body. Second, humans have a *psychological* dimension. We need to consider how our occupation serves the psychological needs of every human, including our social needs. Third, we have a *social* dimension. Our employment needs to provide healthy social bonds and positive community obligations. Our work also provides our primary access to society and community. It helps meet our needs to belong and to feel that we are contributing to something greater than ourselves. Fourth, our occupation reflects the *economic* dimension and provides the financial resources to purchase the goods and services we need and desire. Along with the economic dimension is a *power* dimension both within each organization and among organizations and industries. Finally, Peter believes there is a need to *distribute wealth fairly* within an organization.

[17]Ibid., chap. 2.

[18]Ibid., chap. 36.

[19]Drucker, *Effective Executive*; also Drucker, *Classic Drucker*, chap. 9.

[20]Drucker, *Effective Executive*.

[21]Drucker, *Classic Drucker*, chap. 3. Also Drucker, *Essential Drucker*, chap. 17; Drucker, *Management*, chap. 37. First, classify the problem. Determine if it is a generic problem requiring a rule or principle to guide our decision or an exception to the rule. A generic problem occurs regularly and the organization needs a policy to address it on a consistent basis. An exception to the rule requires our attention and insight in order to come up with a decision that is consistent with our goals and objectives, but falls outside the general guidelines of a stated policy. If at all possible the effective leader wants to be involved in the establishment of the rules and principles that can guide decision making, not simply bogged down in handling exceptions to the rule. Second, define the problem. What is the issue and what must be resolved? What are the specifications that the answer must satisfy? Third, specify what the decision must accomplish and when the answer is needed. Do we need a decision immediately, in a week, by the end of the month, or is it an indefinite time horizon? Fourth, determine what is the "right" solution before entertaining any compromises. In other words, determine the perfect solution before entertaining compromises so that the best alternatives to achieving the desired result can be considered. Fifth, build into the decision the action to carry it out. Who will do it?

When does it need to be done? How will we know we are making effective headway in solving the problem the decision is meant to address? Finally, build feedback loops to test the validity and effectiveness of the decision against real time results.

[22]Drucker, *Effective Executive*, pp. 122-23.

[23]This point was made abundantly clear to me in a conversation a few years ago with Dr. Steve Sample, president of USC. Sample has determined that the CEO/president sets the standard for hiring decisions and that this standard is filtered into every subsequent level of the organization. He reached this conclusion after studying his own hiring through the years as well as through the influence of key economists who had studied workplace hiring. The basic formula is summarized in the section on Sample in chapter three.

[24]Drucker, *Classic Drucker*, chap. 5. Also Drucker, *Essential Drucker*, chap. 9. First, think through the assignment. What are the nonnegotiable qualities of the position and what are the variables? What character traits and threshold competencies must we have in every candidate, and what are personality tendencies that will make the person a high-functioning and preferred member of the team? It is important to keep in mind that we hire for competencies, but fire for attitudes, behaviors and conduct.

Second, look at a number of potentially qualified people. Our opportunity to do this second step will be regulated in part by the hiring culture of our company. If the hiring process is one that we alone control, we will narrow the field quickly. If our hiring culture requires broader buy-in through a search committee, this vetting of several candidates will take time, but is a necessary step in the process. Depending on the assignment, I have hired vice presidents using both methods. Our current vice president of finance, for example, was hired through a targeted approach while the acting provost was hired through a search committee. The culture helped determine the terms and process of these hirings.

Third, the effective leader needs to narrow the field and think hard about the two or three remaining candidates. This is a difficult step, and although I agree that it needs to be done, it often isn't straightforward or easy. In fact, this is one area where I question Drucker's advice because a top candidate is usually resistant to being considered as part of a pool. Often, the top candidates in a search are performing at a high level in their current assignment. They are not looking to leave, and if they have the sense that they will jeopardize their current situation if they pursue this new opportunity then they simply won't do it. It is necessary to take this step in a way that protects their interests while allowing us to evaluate our final candidates against the stated hiring objectives.

Fourth, as we consider the candidates, we discuss each one with people who have worked with them and for them, and who can give us candid feedback on their abilities, tendencies and character. We also need to find people beyond their supplied references who can tell us what they have observed from a distance. This fourth step is both necessary and difficult. This is when we begin to realize what the person will be like in the role. What is the part of their personality that will clash with the job? Can you live with it? I often joke that everyone has 2 percent of their personality that is an outlier, that reflects tendencies or dispositions that require ongoing work. What is this person's 2 percent, how does it show up and under what circumstances?

Finally, when deciding on a finalist, we need to ensure that the person to whom we intend to offer the appointment understands the job, is committed to fulfilling it at a level of high performance and is prepared to accept the offer. At this point, I have found that it is essential to ask, "If you are offered this job and the details of compensation are satisfactory, are you prepared to accept our offer?"

[25]Class notes, MGMT351: The Effective Decision. Finally, to complete our consideration of the central role our people decisions make in the long-term effectiveness and success of the organization, consider Peter's four basic principles of what every people decision must include.

First, if a manager puts a person into a job and he or she does not perform, the manager has made a mistake. The manager is responsible for the performance of the individual. Second, the soldier has a right to competent command. It is the duty of managers to make sure that the responsible people in their organizations perform. Third, people decisions fundamentally determine the performance capacity of the organization. We will never rise higher than our brightest talent. And finally, the one "don't": don't give new people new major assignments, for doing so only compounds the risks. We give this sort of assignment to someone whose behavior and habits we know and who has earned trust and credibility within our organization.

To determine the timing of the decision, consider these following principles: First, what degree of consideration of the future is in the decision being made today? Second, what impact will this decision have on other functions within the organization? Third, what will be the impact of the decision on the conduct, ethical values and social and political beliefs of the organization? Fourth, are decisions recurrent or rare? In other words, are we making decisions over and over again because we have failed to define the principle, or are we confining our decisions to those areas where the entire course of the organization is set?

[26]This allusion is based on the Boston Consulting Group's marketing matrix that features "Problem Children," "Stars," "Cash Cows" and "Dogs" as the four quadrants into which every product in your portfolio must be classified. The goal is to see the problem children become stars, the stars become cash cows and the profits from the cash cows redirected to the problem children, giving them the resources to become stars before the cash cows turn to dogs, thereby becoming a drag on profits.

[27]Drucker, *Essential Drucker*, chap. 11.

[28]Ibid.

[29]Drucker, *Management*, chap. 31, "The Manager and His Work." See also chap. 2 and chap. 4.

[30]For example, as a college president I experience this tension in our personnel policies, our compensation commitments and our fundraising priorities. In considering

our fundraising priorities, for example, there is a constant tradeoff among raising money for the annual fund (money for operations, short-term), raising money for buildings and programs (capital and endowment, mid-term), and raising deferred gifts that will come to the college when a person passes away, which helps build our permanent endowment (long-term). Balancing the allocation of resources to see that the appropriate level of work is done in each area is a challenge.

[31]Drucker, *Management*, chap. 8, "The Power and Purpose of Objectives," and chap. 9, "Strategies, Objectives, Priorities, and Work Assignments." These objectives must derive from the mission and goals of the business. They reflect the fundamental strategy of the organization. They must be capable of being turned into operational objectives. They must help us choose between alternatives, since the opportunities are endless but the resources are scarce. These objectives are needed in every area where performance is crucial for the survival of the business. They cannot encompass everything; therefore, they must encompass what is essential and will focus the concentration of the organization and its resources.

To establish objectives in each area, Peter asks that we determine what are appropriate goals for each area. As we plan, we then need to decide what has to be accomplished to reach these goals and objectives. Finally, we have to integrate the goals and objectives into the overall strategies of the organization by communicating these goals and objectives to the people who are responsible for carrying them out.

The second core operation is to recognize that the effective leader is responsible for organizing the work and activities of the organization, including determining how to make work productive and the worker effective. This is especially challenging and requires our steadfast concentration. Analyzing the internal activities, decisions and external relationships helps establish the order and flow of the work. It helps divide the work into manageable units so that steady progress can be made.

One of the significant challenges I face currently, for example, is organizing the work of our college advancement office as we move deeper into our major capital campaign. As we plan and prepare, we are trying to reach a level of specificity with each job responsibility that will minimize ambiguity and make many of the internal operations capable of assignment to volunteers and professional staff.

Third, an effective leader also sets appropriate benchmarks and measures the success of the specific organization against the leading indicators in his or her field. Drucker is known for having invented the concept of management by objectives (MBO). As noted earlier, MBO works by establishing objectives and benchmarks that determine individual contributions and measure overall success. The unique role of the CEO is to analyze, appraise and interpret individual performance in relationship to the overall needs and goals of the organization.

Fourth, a corollary to our third core operation is Drucker's repeated emphasis that the goal of senior management is to make people productive by cultivating their strengths and neutralizing their weaknesses. He came at this priority from a variety of angles throughout his sixty-year writing career, but it always came down to the same basic formula of determining what results we want and then getting the right people in the right places to see that this occurs. His most original contribution in this area was undoubtedly his insistence that if an individual is ineffective in their current assignment, the manager has made a mistake. On the surface this seems to encourage a level of dysfunction that would be debilitating. What I have come to realize, however, is that Drucker's much more profound point was that the manager had made a mistake in the hiring, in the definition of the job, in the training for successful execution of the work, or in misunderstanding the entire enterprise. This was an entirely new way to consider the task of management.

Fifth, the final core operation of the effective leader is to develop people. This reflects Drucker's great priority and is at the heart of his human-centered approach to leadership. As noted earlier, once we have decided to hire a person, we must take responsibility for his or her current contribution as well as long-term development and success. It is in our management of people at work that we encounter the greatest tests of our integrity and indeed, it is why integrity is so critical for effective leadership.

[32]Each of these core operations requires different qualities and qualifications. When we set objectives, for example, the challenge is to strike the proper balance between alternatives, which requires analytical and synthesizing ability. Conversely, when we organize our task and responsibilities, this requires analytical ability. But because it deals with human beings, it also requires a capacity to understand and empathize with people and their motivations. When we turn to motivating and communicating, we no longer need to analyze as much as we need to integrate and synthesize. Ultimately, each responsibility requires a different constellation of abilities.

[33]Drucker, *Management*, chap. 50. As a result, he refined his understanding by identifying six core tasks as follows. First, the effective leader must think through the mission of the business. This goes to the heart of the questions Drucker taught us to use in every situation. What is your business? What should it be? Who is your customer? What does your customer consider valuable? What is your plan? How will you measure the successful execution of your plan? Answering these questions leads to the setting of objectives, the development of strategies and the making of today's decisions for tomorrow's results.

Second, the effective leader has to set standards, lead by example and be the conscience of the corporation. This in turn raises the whole dimension of the human component in the organization. The effective leader must establish the priorities that ensure people hired into the organization are developed and placed in areas where they can make their greatest contribution, where their strengths are maximized and their weaknesses neutralized.

The third task, developing the human component in the organization, is both the most compelling and the most difficult to fulfill. There are any number of reasons why this is the case. I have never been in an organization that could only play to what a person does best. There is work to do and when pressure comes, nobody believes he or she has enough people to do the work the way he or she prefers to do it. People also have personalities which have very different motive patterns. And what some people consider their strengths are actually the source and cause of some of the most destructive patterns in an organization.

Fourth, in my industry, higher education, smart people with the gift of analysis who also excel at critical thinking surround me. The challenge with this particular gift is that it can develop into a critical spirit that prevents them from separating what they believe they see from how they prefer to work. The result is almost always a numbing spirit of criticism that paralyzes their productivity while limiting their overall effectiveness.

Fifth, it is essential that the effective leader identifies and initiates relationships with the major external constituencies whose interest and support is so critical to the success of the organization. This, in turn, gives rise to the necessity of being comfortable at the countless ceremonial functions we must fulfill as part of the social lubrication of the organization. The importance of cultivating and maintaining external relationships and participating fully in ceremonial functions is often underestimated. Both provide the dynamic interplay that keeps an organization in contact with the various publics they must serve.

Finally, the effective leader must engage in succession planning at two levels: first for the routine successions that occur as a normal part of the business cycle, and then for emergencies that come from accidents or moral failings.

These six tasks are part of the distinct functions of top management and are deployed across twelve essential capacities: (1) a capacity to analyze both internal strengths and external opportunities, (2) a capacity to think through the work of leadership in a disciplined, rational process, (3) a capacity to weigh options and alternatives between different plans and courses of action, (4) a capacity to work with people to harmonize dissent, (5) a capacity to make quick and decisive action possible, (6) a capacity for bold and intuitive courage, (7) a capacity to entertain a variety of abstract ideas, concepts, calculations and figures in order to see multiple options in any given circumstance, (8) a capacity to work with people, including an ability to perceive the basic motive patterns in different individuals, (9) a keen awareness of human nature, (10) a capacity for empathy, awareness and lively interest in and respect for people, (11) a capacity for working alone or in teams, depending what the task requires, and (12) a capacity for fulfilling social obligations where their sheer presence brings the honor and support of the entire organization.

[34]Ibid. Ultimately, Drucker summarized these twelve behaviors into four dynamic temperaments. The effective leader needs to be a "thought man, an action man, a people man, and a front man." A leader also needs to move effortlessly between the temperaments, depending on the context and what he or she determines will best serve the needs of the organization. It is not that this list or any of Drucker's lists were ever meant to be exhaustive. In every case they reflected his latest thinking to date as he both enlarged the range of his understanding and narrowed the scope of what makes for an effective leader.

What is often overlooked, however, is how important it is for a business or organization to remain financially viable. We have to be concerned with profit margins, not because we are greedy but because we need financial margins to run our organizations effectively. One of Drucker's most frequent questions to us was, "What is the first priority of a business?" The answer: to meet the cost of capital so that we can stay in business. It was a completely new way to think about the work and the desired results of every organization.

[35]Drucker, *Classic Drucker*, chap. 7.

[36]The five key questions are: (1) How can we get the effective leader to focus on results rather than activities? (2) How can we get the effective leader to consider how to influence both the present and the future of the organization? (3) How can we get the effective leader to focus on the importance of human relations and the development of the human potential within the organization as the single most significant influence on current and future success? (4) How can we get the effective leader to communicate effectively? (5) How can we accomplish these tasks?

[37]Drucker, *Essential Drucker*, chap. 14.

[38]The following "Six Dysfunctions of the Organization" is based on my personal observation and experience. Some organizations develop recurring problems that prevent them from achieving effectiveness and success. There are at least six primary dysfunctions that contribute to this malaise.

First and most common is the tendency to multiply management levels rather than deal with structural or personnel mistakes. One of the most consistent mistakes I have observed is when we have a person in a role that is not the right fit. Rather than deal with their insufficient performance, we hire around the person in an effort to prop him or her up. I have yet to see this work.

The second dysfunction is failing to address recurring organizational problems. When the same problem keeps coming up, we have a problem in one of three areas: we have the wrong people working on the real problem; we have undercapitalized the solution; or we are working on the right solution to the wrong problem.

The third dysfunction is putting key people on the wrong problems. Remember Drucker's principle that to build effectiveness into the organization we have to put our best people on our biggest opportunities. Often, we siphon off our best people and assign them to problems that nobody else can solve because we are so preoccupied with doing things better that we do not stop to ask whether or not this job should be done at all.

The fourth dysfunction is scheduling too many meetings attended by too many people. Meetings need to have a focus and a purpose. When we invite a person to attend a meeting it needs to be because his or her contribution is needed *and* this person's work on the project is essential. Sometimes meetings proliferate because we aren't sure how to do better what shouldn't be done at all. At other times, meetings proliferate because the organization has been underperforming and needs to get to work.

The fifth dysfunction is when people are more concerned with a person's feelings than with the organization achieving its results. There is an essential need to attend to our core human aspirations to find meaning and purpose through our work. This is fundamentally different than avoiding or minimizing necessary decisions because we are afraid how someone will feel. This is no license to be cavalier in our approach or treatment of people in the organization. Instead, to deal with any situation effectively requires the highest level of respect combined with honesty and transparency about the situation.

The sixth and final dysfunction is when we have too many coordinators or assistants whose job is to support others in their job. This returns us to Peter's bias for lean organizations. It is essential that we determine benchmarks for the number of support personnel essential to do our work. A proliferation of these positions indicates we have not thought through our work and are wasting the resources of the organization. It also indicates a remoteness or disengagement of the people responsible for the work, which in turn leads to ineffective decision making. Often, the overabundance of support personnel indicates either an ambiguity about what needs to be done or an inability to execute the effective decision regarding the mission and direction of the organization.

Principle 3: The Advantage of Team Chemistry
[1]I worked at Azusa Pacific University, Azusa, California, from 1992-2000.

[2]In July of 2000, I became president of Spring Arbor University in Spring Arbor, Michigan. This was my first opportunity to build my own executive team. I learned much through this process, including the importance of hiring smart people who can work together effectively. I immediately realized the necessity of having vice presidents with a strong work ethic, high emotional intelligence and a capacity to build and execute a strategic vision. Ultimately, the capacity to blend a group with vastly different backgrounds into a high-functioning team pursuing a common vision is the responsibility of a leader.

Spring Arbor offered a wonderful challenge. The university has had an uneven history with periods of great growth and development intermingled with periods of significant challenge. When I arrived, the executive team was already in transition. The vice president of finance and the vice president of academics had both left for other institutions. The vice president of enrollment management had arrived just three months earlier, the vice president of advancement was just finishing his second year, and the vice president of student life had been at the institution since the early 1990s. The executive assistant to the president had been moved to another department, and the acting assistant had come out of retirement for a short-term assignment. The transitions occurring within the executive team required that I move quickly to fill these key roles.

Because I enjoy working with people with whom I have had previous success, I began by hiring Brad Sydow, my executive assistant from my previous university. We had worked together for six years. He knew my patterns and pace, and I enjoyed him as a person. As an executive assistant, Sydow helped translate me to the Spring

Arbor culture while also helping translate the Spring Arbor culture to me. Sydow allowed me to be effective immediately because we were so comfortable working together. Often as a new executive settles in, he or she has to learn the key indicators from the culture that can help smooth the transition. Having someone I knew and relied on who was able to build a bridge into a new organization played an indispensable role in my early success.

After securing Sydow's involvement, I moved to fill the vice president of finance role. As I wrote the specifications for the job and considered the complexity of what we would face as an institution, I knew I needed someone who held both an MBA degree and a CPA certification. There was quite a bit of pressure to hire someone the people at Spring Arbor already knew. The candidates that were suggested to me were all strong, but they varied in their preparation, and I was not sure they would be able to fill the role successfully. Then I met Doug Jones.

Jones had been the controller at Huntington College in Indiana. During the interview process, his key references mentioned both his character and his competence. He shared a background similar to that of Spring Arbor, but he had a vastly different path of preparation than any of the other candidates. This contrasting background coupled with a great deal of compatibility gave him an outsider's perspective with an insider's understanding: a winning combination. In August 2000, Jones agreed to join the team at Spring Arbor. When I accepted the invitation to move to Westmont College in 2007, the vice president of finance position at Westmont was open and Jones agreed to come with me for a second run in a new assignment. We have now worked together twelve years.

When I arrived at Spring Arbor, the vice president of advancement was in the midst of finishing his Ph.D. in higher education leadership. Over the next eighteen months, he expressed strong interest in finishing his Ph.D., so during my second year I reassigned him to a different role in order to give him the time he needed to finish his doctoral work, which was his first love. Following completion of his Ph.D., he became provost of another institution. What I learned from this situation is leaders often inherit people who are a great fit for the institution, but are serving in a role not aligned with their first love. As I worked through this situation I often thought of Drucker's emphasis that as we work to ensure the success of those we hire, we must be willing to move them into positions that match their greatest strengths with our most significant needs.

Of course, this change required that I hire a new vice president of advancement and I would come to fill this position with someone who had come out of the financial services industry. This vice president combined an unusual ability with people with a tireless effort to attract resources for the institution. He is also a quick study, and our work together initiated a season of fundraising that helped transform the physical infrastructure of the university.

When I arrived at Spring Arbor, the vice president of student life was the longest serving member of the team. He was near the end of his doctoral program, capable but restless, and interested in becoming a president himself. He left at the end of my second year to become president of a college in the Midwest. He is still in that assignment. I replaced him with his assistant vice president and eventually replaced that individual with another member from the department who is now in her fifth year as vice president of student life. She was an alumna of the university, had worked in the department for several years previously and helped preserve a sense of continuity and momentum as we worked on a variety of growth initiatives.

Hiring a vice president of academics was the most delicate of the new positions. This individual is so critical to the interface with the entire faculty, who in turn are so critical to the success of the institution. We were fortunate to fill this position with a former director of higher education programs at the Kellogg Foundation in Battle Creek, Michigan. She is an outstanding academic administrator and played a key role in helping develop and implement the multiple programs that were started during the seven years I was there.

The vice president of enrollment management was the glue of the team. He served as the barometer for how decisions were working their way through the organization or how challenges were bubbling up from the grass roots. He remains in that role at Spring Arbor and continues to serve a new president with an unusual level of strength and competence.

To this team at Spring Arbor, I added Reed Sheard as vice president of information technology. Eventually, we added a vice president of university communications as well. These new hires were both made in response to acute needs that we faced at the institution. In the case of Sheard, he had spent a number of years in the high tech world and brought a range of gifts and abilities that is rare for an IT person. He too has found his way to Westmont where he is now our vice president of advancement and CIO.

[3]As a result, the development of our executive team at Westmont has been quite different. Rick Pointer has come from within the history faculty to serve as provost and is doing an outstanding job in both program development and personnel management. We needed someone the faculty inherently trusted, who was capable and competent himself, and who could join the team without being a disruptive ego. Rick has excelled on all three fronts. Jane Higa has continued into her twenty-second year as vice president of student life and is a source of great stability and competence. Jane combines a keen understanding of student life programs with a deft hand in interpersonal dynamics and is a great contributor to the team. In addition, Jane is often called on by other institutions to provide counsel and advice as they build effective student life programs. Chris Call, trained as a lawyer, has continued as vice president of administration and planning. This role is built around Chris's unique breadth of gifts and abilities, which are considerable. Chris has been enormously helpful to me on so many fronts, including our work with the community, our interaction with the board of trustees and the general oversight and management of the institution. Doug Jones, former vice president of finance at Spring Arbor, is in his fifth year at Westmont as vice president of finance and continues to oversee all building projects, including more than $100 million in capital improve-

ments. He is a remarkable example of grace and competence. Reed Sheard has done a masterful job of making our technology resources state-of-the-art while accepting the advancement responsibilities accompanying a major capital campaign. Reed is the kind of person that I can give almost any assignment to and he will invest the time and the tenacity to figure out how to make it work so that we can be successful. Cliff Lundberg, a former board member and a veteran of the high tech industry, continues to build the reputation and extend the reach of the college through his work as executive vice president. Cliff has had a lifelong relationship with the college, moving here when he was three, when his father became a professor. He is an alum and has maintained a vast network of Westmont-related people that is a tremendous benefit to the college. Nancy Town, my executive assistant, interprets Westmont culture to me while interpreting me to Westmont culture. She also does a wonderful job of maintaining my effectiveness as a president.

⁴Peter Drucker, *Management: Tasks, Responsibilities, Practices* (New York: Harper & Row, 1973), p. 618.

⁵Ibid.

⁶Ibid., p. 566.

⁷Steven B. Sample, *The Contrarian's Guide to Leadership* (San Francisco: Jossey-Bass, 2002).

⁸Ibid., chaps. 3-4.

⁹Ibid., p. 123.

¹⁰The entire book is worth our attention. His specific treatment of executive teams is found in ibid., pp. 121-39.

¹¹Julie Connelly, "All Together Now," *Gallup Management Journal* 2, no. 1 (2000): 12-18.

¹²Ibid., p. 14.

¹³Daniel Goleman, *Working with Emotional Intelligence* (New York: Bantam Books, 1998).

¹⁴Ibid., pp. 198-231.

¹⁵Ibid., pp. 27-28. The chart on these pages provides a summary of the entire book. Here, in outline form, are Goleman's levels. In his first level, *personal competence*, Goleman identifies the following twelve qualities under three specific categories: (1) Self-awareness: emotional awareness, accurate self-assessment and self-confidence. (2) Self-Regulation: self-control, trustworthiness, conscientiousness, adaptability and innovation. (3) Motivation: achievement drive, commitment, initiative and optimism. The second level, *social competence*, focuses on the engagement of the individual with the broader world where we achieve results. Here, Goleman identifies thirteen qualities under two specific categories. (1) Empathy: understand others, develop others, develop a strong service orientation, leverage diversity and develop political awareness. (2) Social skills: influence by use of tactics of persuasion, communication, management of conflict, leadership, change catalyst, building bonds, collaboration and cooperation, and team capabilities.

¹⁶See Patrick Lencioni, *The Five Dysfunctions of a Team* (San Francisco: Jossey-Bass, 2002). I first worked with this book at Spring Arbor University. The book is a quick

read and features this exercise of developing a shared working agreement among the members of the top management team.

Principle 4: The Interplay of Culture and Context
[1]Ludwig Wittgenstein, *Philosophical Investigations* (Oxford: Blackwell, 1968), pp. 31-32.
[2]Clifford Geertz, *The Interpretation of Cultures* (New York: Basic Book, 1973), p. 223.
[3]James C. Collins and Jerry I. Porras, *Built to Last* (New York: HarperCollins, 1994), pp. 115-39.
[4]Eric M. Eisenberg and Patricia Riley, "Organizational Culture," in *The New Handbook of Organizational Communications*, ed. F. M. Jablin and L. L. Putnam (Thousand Oaks, Calif.: Sage, 2001), pp. 291-319. I have been especially helped by the work and guidance of Dr. Deborah Dunn, professor of communication studies at Westmont College. She has introduced me to several key themes and resources that have greatly enhanced my own understanding.
[5]Ibid., p. 293.
[6]Thomas J. Peters and Robert H. Waterman, *In Search of Excellence* (1982; reprint, New York: HarperBusiness, 2004). This is a landmark study that identified eight key themes of every company in pursuit of excellence: (1) a bias for action, (2) stay close to the customer, (3) autonomy and entrepreneurship, (4) productivity through people, (5) hands-on, value-driven, (6) stick to the knitting—what you know best, (7) simple form, lean staff, and (8) simultaneous loose-tight properties—allowing autonomy with centralized values. Other important works include Terrence E. Deal and Allan A. Kennedy, *Corporate Cultures: The Rites and Rituals of Corporate Life* (1982; reprint, Cambridge, Mass.: Perseus, 2000); and William Bridges, *The Character of Organizations* (Palo Alto, Calif.: Davies-Black, 1992).
[7]Warren Bennis reminds us, "The only viable way to understand organizations is to understand their culture" (Warren G. Bennis, *Organizational Development: Its Nature, Origins, and Prospects* [Reading, Mass.: Addison-Wesley, 1969]).
[8]This taxonomy is developed in Eric M. Eisenberg, H. L. Goodall Jr., and Angela Trethewey, *Organizational Communication: Balancing Creativity and Constraint*, 5th ed. (Boston: Bedford/St. Martin's, 2007). Studies within the *practical* perspective treat culture as an organizational feature that can be managed. They believe they should seek to provide managers with practical advice for improving the culture of their organizations. Books such as *In Search of Excellence* and *Built to Last* are prime examples of research undertaken from this perspective.

The *interpretive* approach rejects the idea that culture can be managed, claiming instead that culture arises from the common behaviors of the members of an organization. Studies from this perspective, which traces its roots to the watershed Alta Conference of 1983, focus on the symbols, stories and discourses that emerge from everyday organizational life.

The *critical and postmodern* grouping reflects the recent trend toward studying power relationships in workplaces. Taking this movement into account, communication scholar Joanne Martin has found that most of today's cultural studies can be characterized as highlighting one of the following: (1) integration, which focuses on consistency and clarity, (2) differentiation, which emphasizes differences and inconsistencies, or (3) fragmentation, which draws attention to the ambiguity that is an inevitable part of modern life. Joanne Martin, *Cultures in Organizations: Three Perspectives* (Oxford: Oxford University Press, 1992).

[9]Martin, *Cultures in Organizations.*

[10]Amitai Etzioni, *The Spirit of Community: Rights, Responsibilities, and the Communitarian Agenda* (New York: Crown, 1993); S. A. Deetz, *Democracy in an Age of Corporate Colonization: Developments in Communication and the Politics of Everyday Life* (Albany: State University of New York Press, 1985).

[11]Dr. Deborah Dunn, "Organizational Culture," unpublished lecture notes, Westmont College, Santa Barbara, Calif., 2009.

[12]In the late 1990s I learned the importance of this lesson directly. During this time I was part of a team working on the development of graduate education in Asia. Toward the end of our negotiations our translator asked if he could speak with me privately. Apparently, in an effort to move the agreement along, one of the members of the other team had offered me a "gift" in hopes of securing my cooperation. Realizing this would not be acceptable to a Westerner, my translator suggested we establish a student scholarship fund as an alternative that would benefit the students who would enroll in the program. Before I could even run the risk of committing a social and cultural faux pas, my translator, who understood exactly what was transpiring crossculturally salvaged the deal and helped us secure the relationship.

[13]David Livermore, *Leading with Cultural Intelligence* (New York: AMACOM, 2010). Ultimately, my own interest in learning "cultural intelligence" and trying to develop a capacity to work crossculturally is twofold. First, every one of us needs to be able to work crossculturally and understand the dynamics of such an undertaking. But we also need to recognize that every time we change companies, we change cultures. We may be in the same country, we may even be in the same town, but a change in organizational culture can be as disorienting as travel to a foreign country.

[14]Used by permission of Harold A. "Red" Poling. Red kept copies of his philosophy of management in his office desk. This copy was given to me during one of our meetings.

[15]To view this video, please go to the website <www.westmont.edu/ebl50/poling video>.

[16]**Allan Gilmour**, vice chairman (retired), Ford Motor Company: "The word *leader* is greatly overused in America, but Red Poling is a real leader. What makes Red so unique is he listens. He listens to the people around him. He picks up views from wherever he can: reading, studying, things of this kind. He has, and I know he'll like these words, a distinction between participation and consensus. He wants people to participate, to give their views; the pluses the minuses, pros and cons, however you want to describe that. But it's not consensus. Not all votes are equal. So he gathers

those views, and then whether he's the boss or someone else is the boss, makes those decisions.

"Next thing I'd say is he doesn't change his mind after he's made the decision. He's consistent. He brings stability to an organization. He would describe it in part as predictability because the part he's responsible for, the whole thing, understands how he looks at things and how he'll continue to do so. To add to that, people say they'd like to find a substitute for hard work, but none of us has been able to find one yet. Very hard worker, very diligent, always did his homework. And you will find that when he comes to meetings he is prepared. He's ready for business."

William Clay Ford Jr., chairman, Ford Motor Company: "Well, I learned a lot from Red. Our styles are very different, but a lot of the things that he stood for are hallmarks of great leadership. Red was very clear in what he wanted for the organization. There was never any question what Red was driving toward. He communicated it well and he was very consistent. The other thing about Red was he was very detail-oriented. Red was very prepared for every meeting, knew every subject, and if you went to a meeting with Red, you better be prepared. And I think the final thing was that Red was very team-oriented. He really didn't care who got the credit; he just wanted to make sure that Ford Motor Company won.

"I think the biggest thing that Red did for Ford was he kept us on a consistent, clear path. Too often in our past, and even recent history, we change our strategic direction; we change our area of emphasis. Red never did that. He was consistent from the day he took the job. The whole organization was aligned behind him because they knew exactly what he wanted and how they fit into that vision. And then he just drove for results and he never deviated. And there were never any surprises with Red. You always knew where he was coming from, you always knew what he expected from you. And I think that really led this company to great success because a company this size can't have too many messages, and a company this size needs to have consistency and Red certainly provided that.

"Wisdom and discipline both are words that immediately leap into your head when you think of Red Poling. He was a great teacher. Red would spend as much time as necessary to explain something to somebody. He was very patient, and if you were new to the job, or new to a subject, he didn't have unfair expectations. Discipline, well that really is the hallmark of Red. He's perhaps the most disciplined person I've ever met. He planned out each day, he planned out each week, he planned out each month, and each year. And the reason I know that is he once showed me his calendar. It was incredible, scared me to death. I thought, my goodness this is what I have to look forward to. But he was very disciplined not only with himself, but with the entire organization, and it really paid off.

"One of the greatest surprises to people when they met Red was what a compassionate, nice man he is. Red was tough. And Red expected results, but Red was never unfair. And when you knew him personally you realized he was a very warm person, very compassionate, and cared deeply about the community in which he lived. I think the biggest element in all of that though is that Red never sought any credit for himself. He was very quick to credit others, and if the Ford Motor Company did well he never used the term *I*. He always would credit everyone around him, and would be the last one to stand forward. And I thought that was very gracious because most CEOs that I've run across can't wait to take the credit. Red let the numbers speak for themselves."

John Devine, former vice chairman, General Motors: "I've had the good fortune to know Red over thirty years so I've seen him up front, and close. I've worked for him. I've worked for him here in the states, in Europe, literally around the world. What stands out with Red in my mind is an absolutely clear focus on where he's going. You get no doubts, and no sideways paths with Red; very clear focus, very clear direction; a strong sense of perseverance. The auto business is a tough business, and you really have this sense that every day is tough and you have to get through it. Red does that extremely well. And then you have to understand his toughness. Again, this is a difficult business and his strength of purpose, his decisiveness, were very important in this business and Red continues to show that to this day."

Carlos Gutierrez, former chairman and CEO, Kellogg Company: "When Red spoke, everyone listened. He always spoke in a soft tone. But I can assure you no one forgot what he said. Another important ingredient is he was able to focus on two or three big things. Too many managers and leaders get focused on ten, fifteen, twenty things. And things become confusing, and you don't really know where to spend your time. I don't think Red ever had that problem. I think he always knew what was important, and what he wanted to focus on. Well I think it's the sense that you can be a very respectful, almost humble individual. But also be incredibly tenacious, tough when he has to be. And those two things don't have to collide, and they don't have to be separate. And I watch Red bring them together into one incredible personality, and one incredible leader. And that's probably the one thing that I still try to emulate."

Dennis Archer, former mayor, city of Detroit, and president of the American Bar Association; currently chairman, Dickinson and Wright: "Red Poling was somebody that I observed long before I became mayor of the city of Detroit. His leadership style was one in which, from my perspective as a lawyer, as a person who reads three or four papers every day, is someone who is always prepared, someone who cared deeply about his employees, about the direction of Ford Motor Company, and took a lot of quiet pride in the cars that were being produced, in the quality of the cars. And I felt that he demonstrated, from someone who did not work with him, a lot of patience, great vision, but someone who was always very thoughtful and very, very well-prepared."

Ralph Babb Jr., chairman and CEO, Comerica Bank: "He has determination. He is always very supportive, and he enjoys what he's doing. And as I listen to the descriptions of the things he's done in business, that very much depicts what I hear. People look up to him. He brings respect when he walks in, and anything he's involved in, in my opinion, has a high level of integrity because he is involved with it. He focuses on the task, thinks it through, gathers the information, and seeks others' counsel.

And then formulates a strategy. And then once that strategy is formulated, there is a great intensity to achieve ultimate goal. And if you think about it, that's the hallmark of a business leader, as well as a leader in any other context."

Gloria Tachuk, assistant to Mr. Poling (retired): "I think everybody felt comfortable with him, working for him. And he was very approachable. I think that was one of the characteristics I admired the most was that he was approachable by every level of the organization. And in fact, early in the 80s when we were at [North American Automotive] he set up a focus group of women to discuss their issues and concerns. He met with them on a monthly basis. They were so impressed by that because they said over the years the secretaries were looked upon as clerks. On the other hand, he said they're a very important part of the company, every job is very important in running the company, whether you're the vice president on the twelfth floor of the world headquarters, or you're sweeping the building. He just treated everybody the same. And I think that's what I admired most about him. I still run into people from Ford today that are still there, and some recently retired. And they always mention Mr. Poling and what a wonderful management team, and how much he did for the company. And they miss him."

[17]Peter F. Drucker, *Management: Tasks, Responsibilities, Practices* (New York: Harper & Row, 1973), chap. 34; Peter F. Drucker, *The Essential Drucker* (New York: Harper-Collins, 2001), chap. 8.

[18]Drucker, *Management*, chap. 19. Most managers, McGregor demonstrated, operate either from a Theory X, where they believe employees are lazy and dislike work, or a Theory Y, where they believe employees have a psychological need to work and derive great satisfaction from achievement and responsibility.

[19]Drucker, *Management*, chap. 20.

[20]Ibid., chap. 21.

[21]Ibid.

[22]Ibid., chap. 32.

[23]Ibid., p. 455.

[24]Ibid., chap. 44.

[25]Ibid., chap. 42.

[26]Ibid., chap. 45.

[27]Ibid., chap. 47.

[28]Ibid., chap. 48.

[29]Ibid., chap. 52.

[30]Drucker, *Essential Drucker*, chap. 5.

[31]Peter F. Drucker, *The New Realities* (New York: Harper & Row, 1989).

[32]Ibid., chap. 9.

[33]Ibid., chap. 14; *Classic Drucker*, chap. 10.

[34]Drucker, *Management*, chap. 11.

[35]Ibid., chaps. 7 and 4.

[36]Robert Wuthnow, *Communities of Discourse* (Cambridge, Mass.: Harvard University Press, 1989).

[37]See appendix 2 for a more extensive treatment.

[38]This study is chronicled in the book by Marcus Buckingham and Curt Coffman, *First, Break All the Rules* (New York: Free Press, 1999).

Principle 5: The Strength of Compatibility and Coherence

[1]Peter Drucker, *The Essential Drucker* (New York: HarperCollins, 2001), chap 15.

[2]Ibid.

[3]Marcus Buckingham and Donald Clifton, *Now, Discover Your Strengths* (New York: Free Press, 2001). See also Buckingham and Coffman, *First, Break All the Rules*. This latter book chronicles the extensive study of 85,000 employees spread across 1,600 companies in which they determined the twelve questions that elicit the qualities of the best places to work. This is the study behind the "Best Places to Work" movement that has swept our nation.

StrengthsFinder identifies thirty-four different talents that an individual might display at work. Marcus Buckingham defines a talent as "a recurring pattern of thought, feeling or behavior that can be productively applied." For ultimate expression and usefulness, talents are to be combined with our accumulated knowledge and our learned skills. This intake instrument is meant to unlock the five dominant themes in our life so we can understand our talents and maximize our contribution. Everyone of us has them.

[4]John D. Beckett, *Loving Monday* (Downers Grove, Ill.: InterVarsity Press, 1998), p. 76.

[5]Ibid., p. 92.

[6]Jim Collins, *Good to Great* (New York: HarperCollins, 2001).

[7]Nat Stoddard and Claire Wyckoff, *The Right Leader: Selecting Executives Who Fit* (Hoboken, N.J.: John Wiley, 2009).

[8]This fit is built on five key components: first, the personal and social competencies of the individual. These cluster around self-awareness, empathy, social expertness, personal influence and mastery of purpose and vision. The second element is having the personality and energy to be fully engaged with the work. Then, the leader must have bedrock character built of trustworthiness and reliability. The fourth element is a keen focus on the needs of the organization, including a careful assessment of the presenting needs versus the real needs. Last comes assessing the fit of the organizational culture with the environmental context. This latter priority dispels several notions, including the ways corporate cultures influence and are influenced by executive leaders.

[9]I have had two executive teams. At Spring Arbor I built the executive team virtually from scratch. Only Matt Osborne, vice president of enrollment, who had been hired the previous fall remained from the team I inherited. Two vice presidents, having been candidates for the position, resigned when I was chosen. Two others would leave during my first two years and two were promoted from within. At Westmont I brought two of my vice presidents from Spring Arbor who have blended in beautifully with the team that was already in place. We have continued to innovate and are still one position away from completely settling the team.

Principle 6: Leading with Convictions

[1] Peter F. Drucker, *Classic Drucker: Essential Wisdom from Peter Drucker from the Pages of "Harvard Business Review"* (Boston: Harvard Business Review, 2006), chap. 11; Peter Drucker, *The Essential Drucker* (New York: HarperCollins, 2001), chap. 15.

[2] C. William Pollard, "Crafting a Culture of Character," *Leader to Leader* 2010, no. S1 (2010):38-42.

[3] Robert Kegan and Lisa Laskow Lahey, *How the Way We Talk Can Change the Way We Work* (San Francisco: Jossey-Bass, 2001).

[4] Ibid., p. 137.

[5] David L. McKenna, *Never Blink in a Hailstorm* (Grand Rapids: Baker, 2005).

[6] Edwin H. Friedman, *Generation to Generation: Family Process in Church and Synagogue* (New York: Guilford, 1985).

[7] McKenna, *Never Blink in a Hailstorm*, pp. 99-100

Principle 7: Maintaining Our Connections

[1] Peter Drucker, *The Essential Drucker* (New York: HarperCollins, 2001), pp. 207-16.

[2] Ibid., p. 10.

[3] Douglas McGregor, *The Human Side of Enterprise* (1960; reprint, New York: McGraw-Hill, 2006).

[4] Drucker, *Essential Drucker*, pp. 80-85.

[5] Ibid., pp. 118-19.

[6] Jean Lipman-Blumen, *Connective Leadership* (New York: Oxford University Press, 1996). The starting point for Lipman-Blumen's work is a critique of the old conventional model of leadership that focused on individualistic, ego-driven accomplishment. It depicted the leader as being out in front, leading the charge, and the organization rising and falling on the leader's every decision. In the new model, a leader is much more embedded in the organization, connected both personally and technologically, and displaying an authenticity, transparency and accountability that inspires confidence.

This new style of leadership is reflective of our human-centered approach. It focuses both on the success and effectiveness of the organization, and the sense of responsibility the organization must carry for its total impact. In other words, the organization is no longer simply focused on economic achievement. As a member of a community it is valued for its total impact—its effect on the environment; its utilization of the vast array of talent, including talent with ethnic and gender diversity; and its impact on society.

In this context, Lipman-Blumen advocates for *connective leadership* because of its emphasis on making connections individually and organizationally that fundamentally address all challenges facing society.

[7] These instruments are the L-BL: Achieving Styles Inventory (ASI), for assessing the individual; L-BL: Organizational Achieving Styles Inventory (OASI), for assessing organizational culture; and Achieving Styles Situational Evaluation Technique

(ASSET), for assessing the fit between an individual and an organization and the achieving styles required by each unique situation.

[8]Lipman-Blumen's qualities and styles are:

1. *Direct* quality: focuses primarily on the tasks that individuals set for themselves.
   - Intrinsic style: where the nature of the task itself motivates us.
   - Competitive style: causes us to want to outdo others.
   - Power style: displayed by our desire to take charge, exert our will or work to confront immediate situations and events.

2. *Relational* quality: reflects an orientation toward helping others achieve their goals.
   - Collaborative style: expressive of an individual's enjoyment of working as part of a member of a team or on joint projects.
   - Contributing style: typified by a person who enjoys helping others complete their chosen tasks.
   - Vicarious style: where a leader derives satisfaction from serving as a mentor and offering wisdom in order to help others accomplish their goals.

3. *Instrumental* quality: reflects a tendency to treat everything and everyone as an instrument for achieving one's goals.
   - Personal style: typified by a leader who draws upon their own intellectual, emotional and personal gifts in order to accomplish their goals.
   - Social style: allows an individual to marshal the goodwill of others through their relational capacity in order to get things done.
   - Entrusting style: leads one to place their hopes and dreams on the ultimate contribution they can make to achieving goals and objectives that are meaningful to the organization.

The contribution of connective leadership is to integrate our personal style, our organizational culture and our environmental context in such a way that the alignment of our achieving style with the culture and the context leads to great results.

[9]Robert J. Emmons, "The Challenge of Leadership," *ABC Roundup*, May-June 2001.

[10]Douglas McKenna, PowerPoint slides from a lecture delivered to Microsoft employees and amplified through several one-on-one executive-coaching sessions (2008–present). In 2000, I was reunited with McKenna, who had years earlier been my undergraduate psychology professor. Today, he is my executive coach and has had a profound impact on my understanding of how convictions and connections work together.

Convictions are our ideas and beliefs. They are our core values. They reflect our calling and mission in life. They influence the way we see, the vision we cast and the confidence we carry in what can be accomplished through our leadership. They reflect the nonnegotiable qualities of our value system. They also reflect the way we will be remembered. Ultimately, they guide us in making tough decisions when confronted with clashing values and competing commitments.

Connections, on the other hand, reflect the way we value other people. Showing respect for another person's convictions and point of view shows an authenticity and openness to others that is a hallmark of an effective leader. It also reflects a mature perspective that recognizes we never make it on our own. It helps us see the priority of learning and listening to others, especially in a fashion that allows us to be responsive without escalating difficult situations.

Convictions and connections operate in dynamic tension with each other. Convictions reflect our principles while connections reflect the priority of other people. When we lose our balance in one direction our convictions lead us to dominate other people. In the other direction our connections cause enabling, codependant behavior. Ultimately learning to balance convictions and connections allows us to be principle-driven while maintaining the integrity of our relationships.

McKenna's articulation and amplification of these principles has guided my own understanding and has helped me recognize the key role the leader plays in the health and vitality of the organization. He has also helped me understand the way that the leader's emotional state sets the tone for the dynamics that develop throughout the organization. If we are able to maintain a sense of composure while articulating our convictions clearly, we will be able to maintain the relational connections that help the organization mature in its capacity and effectiveness. Conversely, if we are always reacting, our negative energy will stifle the creativity and effectiveness of our company. How we maintain our guiding principles without capitulating to our circumstances is so important. Being able to maintain our connections without giving in to dysfunctional patterns will determine our long-term effectiveness and success.

Principle 8: Making an Ultimate Contribution
[1]Peter F. Drucker, *Management Challenges for the 21st Century* (New York: Harper-Collins, 1999).
[2]Dennis Hagen, a research paper prepared for Practicum for Superintendents, taught by Dr. Phil Piele, School of Education, University of Oregon, spring semester 1987. The paper is available on request.

Appendix 1
[1]Henri Fayol, *General and Industrial Management* (London: Pitman, 1949).
[2]Chester I. Barnard, *Functions of the Executive* (Cambridge, Mass.: Harvard University Press, 1938). Also Philip Selznick, *Leadership in Administration: A Sociological Interpretation* (New York: Harper & Row, 1957).
[3]Henry Mintzberg, *The Nature of Managerial Work* (New York: Harper & Row, 1973). The interpersonal roles of *figurehead*, *leader* and *liaison* are typified by an external focus of the leader's activities. The *figurehead* is obligated to perform a number of routine duties of a legal or social nature. The *leader* is responsible for the motivation and activation of subordinates and for staffing, training and associated duties. The *liaison* maintains networks of outside contacts and sources of information that help to provide an external perspective for the organization.

The informational roles of *monitor*, *disseminator* and *spokesperson* have an internal focus. The *monitor* seeks and receives broad input that provides an extensive understanding of the organization and the environment in which it operates. The *disseminator* transmits this information throughout the organization. The *spokesperson* transmits internal information externally, telling the outside world the appropriate level of information regarding company strategies and plans.

Finally, the decisional roles of *entrepreneur, disturbance handler, resource allocator* and *negotiator* help build bridges between the internal work of the organization and the external environment in which the organization must achieve results. The *entrepreneur* is able to see new possibilities and marshal the resources to pursue them. The *disturbance handler* is able to handle disruptions to the product line as well as the external environment. The *resource allocator* looks inward and outward, and balances internal capacity with external opportunity. Finally, the *negotiator* has to balance competing commitments to ensure that all compromises preserve the quality and integrity of the product while creating the circumstances for a win-win solution for all involved.

[4]Morgan W. McCall and Cheryl A. Segrist. *In Pursuit of the Manager's Job: Building on Mintzberg* (Greensboro, N.C.: Center for Creative Leadership, 1980); Lance B. Kurke and Howard E. Aldrich, "Mintzberg Was Right! A Replication and Extension of the Nature of Managerial Work," *Management Science* 29, no. 8 (1983): 975-84; Anne S. Tsui, "A Role Set Analysis of Managerial Reputation," *Organizational Behavior and Human Performance* 34 (1984): 64-96; and John P. Kotter, *The General Managers* (New York: Free Press, 1982).

[5]Sydney Finkelstein, Donald C. Hambrick and Albert A. Cannella Jr., *Strategic Leadership: Theory and Research on Executives, Top Management Teams, and Boards* (New York: Oxford University Press, 2009). These three categories are *external and internal activities; strategy formulation, implementation and context creation;* and *substance and symbols.* Finkelstein emphasizes that top executives are the link between the *internal* world of the company and the *external* environment where the company must achieve results. The CEO conveys information about the company to external audiences while carrying information from the outside world back to the company in order to incorporate this new information, new technologies, market trends and recurring regulatory forces (etc.) into the strategy of the company. Other key activities of the top executive include engaging in *strategy formulation, implementation and context creation.*

[6]Isaac Ansoff, *Strategic Management* (1965; reprint, New York: Palgrave MacMillan, 2007). I have found his articulation of the role of the CEO to be important in understanding my own work as a college president. The opportunity I have as a president to shape the strategy of my organization is enormous. Both through my own decisions and through the authority distributed to my vice presidents and others, I help determine the performance capacity of our organization.

I am deeply engaged, for example, in the strategic planning process without having to do all the work. It is critically important that I participate fully and that I lend my full support to its development and execution. Nevertheless, it is a process that clearly has to be owned and embraced by the entire college and not just by the top management team or by myself.

Finkelstein's main thrust is to demonstrate that top executives engage in a wide array of roles, responsibilities and practices in order to achieve success for their companies through effective leadership.

[7]Jeffrey Pfeffer, *Power in Organizations* (Boston: Pitman, 1981). Also, Thomas Dandridge, Ian Mitroff and William F. Joyce, "Organizational Symbolism: A Topic to Expand Organizational Analysis," *Academy of Management Review* 5, no. 1 (1980): 77-82.

[8]Finkelstein, Hambrick and Cannella, *Strategic Leadership;* Mintzberg, *Nature of Managerial Work.*

[9]Sydney Finkelsetin, "Power in Top Management Teams: Dimensions, Measurement, and Validation," *Academy of Management Journal* 35 (1992): 505-38.

[10]Finkelstein, Hambrick and Cannella, *Strategic Leadership,* p. 123.

[11]Patrick Lencioni, *The Five Dysfunctions of a Team* (San Francisco: Jossey-Bass, 2002). Lencioni identifies the five dysfunctions of a team as (1) absence of trust, (2) avoidance of conflict, (3) lack of commitment, (4) avoidance of accountability and (5) inattention to results. He then counters these five dysfunctions with five functions of a healthy team: (1) trust one another, (2) engage in open and dynamic dialogue, (3) commit to decisions and plans of actions, (4) hold one another accountable for achieving results and (5) focus on achievement of collective results.

[12]Charles A. O'Reilly III, Richard C. Snyder and Joan N. Boothe, "Executive Team Demography and Organizational Change," in *Organizational Change and Redesign,* ed. George P. Huber and William H. Glick (New York: Oxford University Press, 1993), pp. 147-75.

[13]Finkelstein, Hambrick and Cannella, *Strategic Leadership,* pp. 139-43.

[14]Ibid., p. 126.

[15]Dan R. Dalton and Idalene F. Kesner, "Organizational Performance as an Antecedent of Inside/Outside Chief Executive Succession: An Empirical Assessment," *Academy of Management Journal* 28, no. 4 (1985): 749-62.

[16]Donald C. Hambrick and Phyllis Mason, "Upper Echelons: The Organization as a Reflection of Its Top Managers," *Academy of Management Review* 9 (1984); Katherine J. Klein and Robert J. House, "On Fire: Charismatic Leadership and Levels of Analysis," *Leadership Quarterly* 6 (1995); Patricia Pitcher and Anne D. Smith, "Top Management Team Heterogeneity: Personality, Power and Proxies," *Organization Science* 12, no. 1 (2001); Albert A. Cannella Jr. and Tim R. Holcomb, "A Multi-Level Analysis of the Upper Echelons Model," in *Multi-Level Issues in Strategy and Methods,* ed. Alfred Dansereau and Francis J. Yammarino, Research in Multi-Level Issues (Oxford: Elsevier, 2005), pp. 197-237.

Appendix 2

[1]See, for example, *The Federalist Papers* 10, where James Madison articulates the great challenges facing American democracy as it seeks to integrate people from all walks of life into a nation governed by the "rule of law."

ANNOTATED AND GENERAL BIBLIOGRAPHY

Drucker Texts

Drucker, Peter F. *The Effective Executive.* New York: Harper & Row, 1966.

The job of the leader is to be effective; that is, to get the right things done. Effectiveness can and must be learned. Effective executives know where their time goes; they focus on outward contribution; they build on strengths; they concentrate on the few major areas where superior performance will produce outstanding results; and they make effective decisions. Drucker discusses each of these concepts and shows how an executive can become effective by accomplishing them.

Drucker, Peter F. *Management: Tasks, Responsibilities, Practices.* New York: Harper & Row, 1973.

This is Drucker's largest and most comprehensive book. Written in 1974 and updated several times, it covers the beachfront in terms of issues and challenges for executive leadership, spanning several hundred pages. For the purposes of writing this text, I ended up reordering the chapters according to the eight principles of effective leadership. Still, as we read the book, we quickly realize the major themes and overlapping concerns that Drucker covers: managing ourselves, the rise and role of the knowledge worker, understanding our organizational culture and environmental context, the overarching competencies we need to be effective and the necessity that we perform and achieve the results necessary to lead our company to success. There are several chapters that do not fit easily within any of the eight principles, but they still amplify key themes that Drucker returned to throughout his writing career.

Drucker, Peter. *Management Challenges for the 21st Century.* New York: HarperCollins, 1999.

Published in 1999, this Drucker classic focuses on the challenges executives face in understanding their context at the same time as they are responsible to craft a coherent strategy. At the heart of this volume is the reality that basic paradigms for understanding reality are shifting, and with this shift comes the necessity that leadership and management shift as well. Summarizing such broad topics as strategy, performance and change, Drucker elaborates on the challenges confronting the global society at the turn of the twenty-first century. Noting such significant shifts as the transition in information technology from being tactical to being strategic, Drucker notes the way technology is shifting the entire landscape of business. At the rise of the twenty-first century, Drucker anticipated that the Internet would be the driving force of global commerce and that our interconnectivity would foster unprecedented opportunities for innovation and change. The book concludes with two key chapters on two enduring themes: how to make the knowledge worker productive, and the necessity of learning to manage ourselves in the new economy, both Drucker classics.

Drucker, Peter. *The New Realities.* New York: Harper & Row, 1989.

A book about understanding the context we find ourselves in. The opening chapter deals with reading history and recognizing the divide that was crossed somewhere between 1965 and 1973. Almost every discipline now acknowledges that this was a time of great turbulence and change. The book contains a wonderful exposition of the challenges facing every major country and economy at the end of the twentieth-century. With chilling irony the book's release chronicling Drucker's prediction of the demise of the Soviet Union coincided almost precisely with its actual demise. Of course, he was no prophet. Drucker's capacity to read the macro- and microeconomic factors impacting every economy as well as balancing the economic indicators with a keen sense of human nature fostered his sense that the Soviet Union, as we had known it, was doomed. The book concludes with several compelling observations about what lies ahead and the challenges and opportunities coming in virtually every sphere of society (social, political, economic, religious, cultural, legal and educational).

Drucker Anthology

Drucker, Peter. *Classic Drucker: Essential Wisdom from Peter Drucker from the Pages of "Harvard Business Review."* Boston: Harvard Business Review, 2006.

This anthology consists of fifteen chapters, all of which appeared separately in the *Harvard Business Review.* The book begins with the enduring theme that today's knowledge worker must learn to manage him- or herself. It then moves into various ways we understand the external environment, the role and responsibilities of business within it, and the work of the senior executive, who must function effectively. Managing other people, making effective decisions, engaging innovation and managing for effectiveness, four of the key themes presented here, recur in a variety of places throughout his sixty-plus-year writing career, and represent some of his finest thinking on the work of effective executives. The book's closing chapters highlight a variety of challenges that lie ahead, what type of knowledge the executive will need and the shift from a society of individual and discrete businesses to a new society defined by huge, sprawling corporations with multinational benefits and impacts. This book is a helpful introduction to key themes and enduring principles found throughout Drucker's writings.

General Bibliography of Other Drucker Texts

Drucker, Peter F. *Concept of the Corporation.* New York: New American Library, 1964.

———. *The Essential Drucker.* New York: HarperCollins, 2001.

———. *Innovation and Entrepreneurship: Practice and Principles.* New York: HarperCollins, 1985.

———. *Management Cases.* New York: Harper & Row, 1977.

———. *Managing for the Future: The 1900s and Beyond.* New York: Truman Talley Books/Plume, 1993.

———. *Managing for Results: Economic Tasks and Risk-taking Decisions.* New York: Harper & Row, 1964.

———. *Managing the Nonprofit Organization: Principles and Practices.* New York: HarperCollins, 1990.

———. "On the CEO's Work." Excerpts from a "Thoughtful Conversation," delivered on October 1, 2004, hosted by the Peter F. Drucker Research Library and Archive. *The Claremont Graduate University Flame,* spring 2005, pp. 24-25.

———. *Post-Capitalist Society.* New York: HarperCollins, 1993.

———. "The Culture of Competence: Managing, Marketing, Motivating, and Missions." *Success,* September 1989, p. 16.

Drucker, Peter F., with Joseph A. Maciariello. *The Daily Drucker.* New York: HarperCollins, 2004.

Other Relevant Texts

Bennis, Warren. *On Becoming a Leader.* Reading, Mass.: Addison-Wesley, 1989.

This book revolves around the assumptions that leaders are made, not born, and that leaders are able to express themselves fully. Bennis stresses the importance of first mastering the context, understanding the basics and knowing oneself and the world. He then discusses the leader's abilities to operate on instinct, deploy him- or herself, and how to move through chaos and get people on his or her side. Finally, he presents his thoughts on organizations and the future of leadership. All of these topics are addressed with the goal in mind of fully expressing oneself.

Blanchard, Kenneth, and Spencer Johnson. *The One Minute Manager: How to Give Yourself and Others the "Gift" of Getting Greater Results in Less Time.* La Jolla, Calif.: Blanchard-Johnson, 1981.

Most managers are said to be either too results focused or too people focused. This is the story of a young man, searching for the middle ground between the two, who meets the "one minute manager" and learns the concepts of one minute goal setting, one minute praisings, and one minute reprimands. Goal setting is done to make expectations clear to both managers and employees; praisings are used to point new employees in the right direction; and reprimands are used to correct the behavior of those who are more experienced.

Collins, Jim. *Good to Great: Why Some Companies Make the Leap . . . and Others Don't.* New York: HarperCollins, 2001.

Presents the findings of a five-year research project that sought to uncover the universal distinguishing characteristics that cause a company to go from good to great. Eleven good-to-great companies that underwent transformations and sustained greatness for at least fifteen years are compared to eleven direct-comparison companies that did not undergo transformations. The results indicate that the good-to-great companies shared characteristics such as the presence of a Level 5 leader, a focus on *who* before *what*, an ability to confront the brutal facts, a "Hedgehog Concept," a culture of discipline, technology accelerators and more.

De Pree, Max. *Leadership is an Art.* New York: Dell, 1989.

Leadership is much more of an art than a set of things to do. De Pree presents his thoughts on artful leadership, which he developed during his tenure at Herman Miller, in this series of ideas and stories. Topics discussed include participative management, the value of diversity, the rights of workers, roving leadership, intimacy, tribal storytelling, the interception of entropy, performance reviews, being abandoned to the strengths of others, choosing leaders, communication, equity, contribution and more.

Goldsmith, Michael. *What Got You Here Won't Get You There: How Successful People Become Even More Successful.* New York: Hyperion, 2007.

Goldsmith argues that previous success often prevents people from achieving further success because the good results of their past behaviors cause them to resist making the changes necessary to achieve further success. Twenty-one habits are discussed, all but one of which are annoying interpersonal issues. Finally, Goldsmith introduces a process for changing those behaviors, which includes feedback, apologizing, advertising, listening, thanking, following up and practicing feed forward.

Kotter, John. *Leading Change.* Boston: Harvard Business School Press, 1996.

Kotter lists the eight main reasons why firms fail and shows how firms can create successful change by avoiding those errors. The positive behaviors in the eight-step process toward successful change are (1) establishing a sense of urgency, (2) creating a guiding coalition, (3) developing a vision and strategy, (4) communicating the change vision, (5) empowering broad-based action, (6) generating short-term wins, (7) consolidating gains and producing more change, and (8) anchoring new approaches in the culture. Kotter also discusses the organization of the future and lifelong learning.

Maxwell, John C. *The 21 Irrefutable Laws of Leadership: Follow Them and People Will Follow You.* Nashville: Thomas Nelson, 1998.

This list of the essential things John C. Maxwell has learned about leadership includes discussions of leadership ability, effectiveness, influence, daily processes, navigation, planning, listening, trust, respect, intuition, magnetism, connection, executive teams, empowerment, raising up other leaders, vision, victory, momentum, priorities, sacrifice, timing, growth and legacy. Each of the laws presented discusses one of these topics and illustrates the law with several real-life examples or models.

Sun Tzu. *The Art of War.* Trans. Lionel Giles. London: Luzac, 1910.

This classic military treatise, written in China during the 6th century B.C., discusses the laying of plans, waging war, the sheathed sword, the weak and strong points of an army, maneuvering, variation of tactics, the army on the march, dealing with different types of terrain, when and when not to fight, attack by fire, and the use of spies. Although originally written as a guide for military generals, this work is now frequently used by business managers and other leaders to make sense of contemporary competitive situations.